# How to Outlive Your Lifetime!

# HOW TO OUTLIVE YOUR LIFETIME!

Preserving a Place in Your Family's Hearts and History

## Timothy W. Polk

FAMILY LIFE INTERNATIONAL

*To*
*Gyoconda and Alexandra,*
*who make every day a holiday*
*and every meal a feast.*

Family Life International books may be purchased for educational, business, or association/society use. For information, call or write: Special Projects Manager, Family Life International, P.O. Box 2803, Sunnyvale, CA 94087. Telephone: (408) 730-0831.

Editor: Bev Manber
Cover design: Jeff Holmes
Illustrations: Michele Smith

Printed in the United States of America

Library of Congress Catalog Card Number: 94-8759

ISBN: 0-9640587-0-7

0 1 0 3 0 4 0 1 5 0

# Contents

# Preface

## This Book's Mission

In writing this book, I am hoping to inspire and empower people to preserve parts of their life for themselves and future generations.

## This Book's Vision

This book is based on a few simple ideas. They are as follows:

1.  Your life *is* interesting. We often fail to give importance to our own life story. We are each an integral element in the continuing saga of our ancestors' and descendants' histories, the connector that ties the past and future together, the one that gives continuity to our family's traditions and ties.

2.  It's up to you to preserve and share parts of your life. No one else can record and remember your actions, thoughts and feelings as accurately as you do.

3.  While there are many books dedicated to researching and preserving the past, no real guide exists on ways to save a part of your life, what I call "preserving the present."

4.  As you consciously attempt to record and preserve parts of your life, you will be inspired to live a better, more meaningful life. While being remembered in your family's history is important, being remembered in their hearts is more so.

*How To Outlive Your Lifetime!* is designed as a starting point, a catalog of ideas for you to expand or modify, based on your interests. Hopefully you will find that many of the ideas are very simple, fun and worth doing.

Please note you certainly don't have to do each idea or project mentioned. The goal is not to save your entire world, just a tiny part of it. Follow through on the suggestions that interest you and spark your interest. Even taking action on only one item would be worthwhile.

I do suggest you try to do as many as possible. Your goal is to paint a complete a picture of your life, using as many different colors as possible.

I also encourage you to view this book as one (maybe your first!) gift you can give to the future. Think of this as your mini-diary or workbook. Do the exercises, record your thoughts and pertinent family history information, make notes in the margins. Someone, someday, will find your thoughts fascinating.

This book isn't just for family history researchers. Whether or not you've previously found information on any of your ancestors, you should preserve parts of your life. Do it for yourself. Do it for your children. Do it for those of the future.

---

**♦ EXERCISE:**
**A simple way to start preserving part of your life is to write your name in all the books you own. For example, on the title page of this book—the first page as you open the cover—in the upper right-hand corner, write your name, today's date, and the city, state and country you are in at this moment. This assumes, of course, this book is yours. If it isn't, you may purchase a copy either by visiting your local bookstore or by using the order form at the back of this book.**

---

## Why I Wrote This Book

Around the world there are millions of people researching their family histories, either professionally or as a hobby. These people are passionate about researching, preserving and honoring the past.

Family history research is a noble effort, and I am proud to do it. I've been researching my family history off and on for more than ten years. My discoveries have astounded me. I've found relatives I never knew I had. I've located a farmhouse that was built by my third-great-grandfather in 1836, tucked away in the rolling fields of southern Ohio. I've traveled to Europe and walked through the towns, churches and graveyards of my European ancestors.

My family research has been an incredibly fascinating adventure, and I look forward to what new discoveries lie ahead. As I've learned about my past, I've also learned about myself.

In doing my research, however, I have been troubled by a feeling that something is missing. And that feeling has developed into an idea I've put into practice during the past several years, which has become the premise of this book: while it is important to research and preserve the past, it's equally important to leave something of our lives behind for future generations. We must preserve part of our lives, the today, the "burning ember" that makes us who we are.

Thus, this book is the book that I wish my parents, grandparents and ancestors had read and used. My suggestions are based on my experiences as well as my discussions with various people and organizations. I'm attempting to light the fire and show you how to make that fire burn brightly once it is ignited.

There are many positives to this idea of preserving parts of your life. It's easy to do and takes little time. It certainly isn't costly—although, like any hobby, you can spend as much money as you like. And it offers a tremendous amount of fun and satisfaction both for yourself and for future generations. This can easily turn into a cause that lasts a lifetime. And, it's a cause I believe will outlive your lifetime!

In addition to being a guide for others, this book is something I can leave behind showing a picture of my life. I have purposely used my real life names, dates and places in the examples to record parts of my life. While these examples are colored by my religious, cultural and educational backgrounds, you can modify the suggestions based on your own beliefs and ideas.

Does this sound ambitious? I have purposely tried to make the scope of this book as wide as possible, both to stretch myself and because the subject—a person's place in history—is so broad. My aim has been to create a personal guide for you to use as a starting point on your journey to outlive your lifetime.

## What's Ahead

Part 1, "Preserving the Present," describes why preserving parts of your life is important.

Part 2, "Delighting Your Descendants," provides practical tips on starting.

Part 3, "Making Your Mark," gives insights and ideas on ways to make your mark in this world.

Part 4, "Finding Your Family History," provides information on how to begin family history research (because family research is so closely linked to preserving information about your life).

Appendix A recaps this book and offers an outline on possible ways to proceed.

Two other important sections are those entitled "Organizations Mentioned in This Book" and "Related Books Worth Reading." Please note that information on how to contact or find the organizations and books mentioned throughout the text are listed in these two sections.

## How to Get the Most Out of This Book

This book is a blueprint for action. I encourage you to do the following to get the most out of this book:

- *Read selectively*. Go through the book once, reading what catches your attention. Later, after you have digested some of the ideas, reread thoroughly sections you skimmed over.

- *Read aggressively*. Underline key passages, write notes in the margins, mark special pages, review highlighted items more than once.

- *Participate actively*. This book is meant to be interactive. Fill in the blanks when asked. Mark the checklists. Do the exercises. Participating is an essential part of the learning process.

## Send Me Your Feedback

I would enjoy learning your thoughts and ideas after you read this book. Was it helpful? Are you dedicated to or at least interested in recording, sharing and perpetuating parts of your and your family members' lives? What other tips can you share that I might pass along in future editions? Are there other products (newsletters, other books, etc.) you think would be helpful?

Thanks for your input. It is sincerely appreciated.

Tim Polk
c/o Family Life International
P.O. Box 2803-01
Sunnyvale, CA 94087

# PART 1

## Preserving the Present

# CHAPTER 1

# Why Do Anything?

*The happiest moments of my life have been the few*
*which I have past at home in the bosom of my family.*
*—Thomas Jefferson*

I arrived home from work and there on the kitchen table sat a package. I hurried over and my excitement was confirmed: it was the reply I had been waiting for from the National Archives in Washington, D.C.

I picked up the package and its bulkiness made my heart race. Inside was information on my third-great-grandfather, who fought for the North in the Civil War. He, his pregnant wife, and two sons journeyed to America from Germany in 1852. Less than ten years later, at the age of 53, he was fighting in the most deadly war the world had ever known.

Carefully opening the package, I took out the ten or so papers inside. My anticipation was rewarded. The Archives' records painted an amazing picture of my grandfather, giving a description of his physical appearance, listing the battles he fought in and detailing his discharge after two years of service because of medical problems. And included was an invaluable (to me) piece of my third-great-grandfather: his signature on a pension application.

## The Forgotten Past

Those of us who do family history research know the joy of discovering information about a relative. It can be exhilarating to find a part of our family's past.

One reason for this is that, generally speaking, there is little of the past to find. While doing my family research, I've been amazed at how little I've been able to find out about some of my ancestors and relatives. Aside from mention in a census report or a birth or marriage or death certificate stashed away in a courthouse, there just isn't that much information available about most people. Information of a personal nature often only exists if a person was famous or wrote letters.

The scary part to me is that this is also true for people who lived fairly recently.

My great-grandfather, William Polk, is an example. He was born in Cleveland, Ohio, in 1909 and died forty-three years later in the same city. Despite the fact that he had seven children and more than ten grandchildren, I can find almost nothing of a personal nature about his life. I know when and where he was born, where he worked his entire life, the date of his marriage, the names of his kids, and when and where he died and is buried. And that is it. I don't know anything about the man himself.

The sad part is that I'll probably never know. His generation is gone now, and the generations that have followed know little and remember even less. I am constantly amazed at how quickly people forget and how time erases generations. William Polk died less than forty years from the date I am writing this, and yet it is almost—almost—as if he never existed.

## Some Reasons Why

Following are three reasons that motivate me to preserve parts of my life. I believe one or more will motivate you, too.

### Reason 1: For Posterity

A compelling reason for taking action to preserve parts of your life is this: by leaving something of yourself behind, you achieve a form of immortality.

We are all going to die one day. Why not leave something of your life behind for your relatives and for, quoting Alex Haley's words in his book *Roots*, "those waiting to be born"? Wouldn't it be wonderful if there was a record of your life, something that outlives you, something that never dies? And this record would do more than just record dates and major events; it would also show and/or tell what type of person you were; what things, people and places excited you; what you spent your free time doing.

I believe that this is the most compelling reason to preserve parts of your present life. It is too easy to lead a long life complete with children and grand-children, and then be forgotten twenty or ten or even five years after your death. I'm seen this many times when doing family history research. Very few people have buildings named after them, or write a critically acclaimed book, or produce great paintings. You and I, the "average" people, need to take efforts to make sure something of our lives outlives us.

Why bother leaving something behind for posterity?

I can almost guarantee that sometime in the future one of your relatives will try to discover what you were like and what your life was about. Who will want to research your life? Hopefully your kids; more likely it will be your grandchildren. Even if you don't have children, it is likely that one day a distant second cousin once or twice removed will want to know more about you and your life.

Leaving something of your life behind would be a wonderful gift that you could give future generations. Think of the joy and excitement your descendants and relatives will have when your records and mementos are discovered.

Have fun with this. Explain in a one-page note how you were kicked out of college or received a traffic ticket. Write a letter to your great-grandson or daughter advising him or her who to vote for in the year 2040. Record on audio how you met your spouse, and what attracted him or her to you. Leave a puzzle behind about some aspect of your life complete with clues and a solution. Hide a "treasure," mention it in your will, but don't say *where* it's located. The possibilities are endless.

You also can record an accurate account of your life. Many autobiographies are written today, not out of a desire to write, but out of a need to "set the record straight." Your life is unique. Only you can accurately depict your life and what you have seen, felt and experienced. A good, albiet extreme, example of this is Holocaust victims who are writing down their experiences—they don't want the world to forget what took place.

Also, preserving a part of your life now will help you connect with the future. Family members share a common bond despite differences of generations or distance. Wayne Dyer, a noted author and speaker, calls this connection an "invisible thread" running through each of our lives that links us together.

Remember, you are the link between the past and the future. The critical question to ask yourself is, "Will I be a strong link or a weak link?"

## Reason 2: To Enhance Your Present Life

I am convinced that preserving and recording parts of your life will enhance and strengthen the relationships you have with family members and friends. As these important people get to know you better, as they learn more about your life, you will find yourself able to build deeper, more lasting relationships.

These days relatives live far from each other. It is getting more and more difficult to know your grandparents, aunts and uncles, cousins. By preserving a part of your life and sharing it with family and friends, you help tear down the walls that distance and time so effectively erect.

I suggest that you pick one or two people who are important in your life and dedicate your preservation efforts to them. In my case, it is my two-year-old daughter, Alexandra. I want her to know all she can about her mother, father and relatives, including, of course, important dates and places, but also what they were and are like as people, as human beings. A significant part of my interest in preserving the present is my desire to live a life Alexandra would be proud of, and to leave a part of me behind so that she will know me better.

---

♦ **EXERCISE:**
**Pick one person, real or imaginary,[1] who you want to designate as the primary person to whom you will leave a part of your life. Write down this person's name:**

---

## Reason 3: For Yourself

A third reason to preserve a part of your life is that this effort will more than likely motivate you to lead a better life. You'll feel better about yourself and your contributions to the world during your brief stay on this planet.

Part 3 of this book presents a concept I call "Making Your Mark." If you take the time to preserve a part of your life, you will want to preserve those "good" things you did. In other words, you will want to lead a life that's *worth* preserving.

---

[1] Many people think of a yet-unborn relative.

# PART 2

## Delighting Your Descendants

# CHAPTER 2

# Basic Ideas

*There are places we all come from—*
*deep-rooty-commonplaces—that make us who we are.*
*—Robert Fulghum*

Who we are, where we have come from, and our goals and aspirations for the future are important things to share both with family members living and with those not yet born.

Like most hobbies, preserving parts of your life can be as simple or as complex as you make it. Chapters 2 through 4 explore various ideas that you can use to record and share your life. You can begin implementing many of the suggestions almost immediately with little or no expense. Others will require greater time and financial investments.

Do not attempt to do all of the ideas mentioned. Simply do what most appeals to your interests, time and financial capacities. Over time, you can revisit this section and complete other projects.

---

**♦  NOTE:**
**When completing any of the ideas or projects mentioned in this book, always keep the word "quality" in mind. You are attempting to preserve and share important pieces of your life that hopefully will last for years to come. With this in mind, invest in high quality materials that complement and protect. For example, you would be better off spending a little extra money to purchase a quality photo album that will protect your photos rather than a "cheap" album that over time will yellow and harm your precious pictures.**

---

## If You Do Nothing Else

Keep a folder or envelope of various miscellaneous items about parts of your life. Include items that you think future generations will enjoy and/or benefit from.

The folder doesn't have to be fancy. I recommend that you buy one that has a cover that can be closed. It would be difficult to spend more than a few dollars on this folder or envelope.

Fill your special "personal preservation folder" with items that give a brief glimpse of you and your life. These "things" can be originals or copies. Originals are best, although some, like a passport, should remain in a safety deposit box. Almost everything you include will have some interest to future generations. Think of your folder as a combination scrapbook, photo album, and important-paper file.

Here are some items perfect for your folder:

- Birth, marriage and death certificates.
- Job reviews
- Loan applications
- Letters from relatives
- Pictures of your family
- Golf scorecards
- Your résumé
- Cancelled checks
- Old appointment books
- Telephone and address books
- Valentine's and other cards from your kids
- Letters, particularly love letters
- Old posters
- Bank statements
- Copies of your tax return
- Paycheck stubs

Does this sound too simple? Maybe, but over time it is highly effective if you continue to add a variety of items. I wish my ancestors had kept something similar to help me get a better feel for their lives.

What other items can you include? Just about anything you feel paints a picture, no matter how small, about yourself and your life. Items family researchers, in particular, find valuable, and which would be interesting to anyone include:

- Anything that is signed by you and dated
- The address of where you lived at a particular time
- Financial matters, such as how much money you make
- Humorous items, such as traffic tickets, a notice for jury duty, over-the-hill cards you received for your fortieth birthday, etc.

The great thing about your folder is that it is almost impossible to go wrong. Everything you include should be of interest to future generations.

Remember, too, that every item you include does not have to be an all-encompassing landscape of your life. Think of your preservation folder as a box that holds a jigsaw puzzle of your life. Each item, by itself, is interesting; but only when the pieces are put together can someone get a clear picture of what you were like and what your life was like.

### Items in My Folder

These are some of the items that I have in my folder:

- A receipt listing books I purchased from the Book-of-the-Month club
- One of my "to-do" lists
- A golf card from a round I played with three other friends
- An itinerary from a business trip
- A receipt for wine purchased from Bonny Doon Vineyard
- A blank check from an old account
- An old list of address and telephone numbers
- A ticket stub from my visit to Fenway Park
- An invitation to my daughter's first birthday party

## Other Storage Options

Your preservation folder doesn't have to be a folder. Documents and personal items can be preserved in boxes, scrapbooks, photo albums, envelopes and notebooks, to name a few possibilities. Another good idea is to have a drawer or bookshelf devoted to your "treasures."

You also may want to have a separate storage item for each family member. This would be especially true if you have young children and can add mementos from throughout their childhoods.

## Think of Your Children

A quick way to judge if something should be included in your folder is to ask yourself this simple question: "Would my children (grandchildren) find this piece of my life interesting?"

---

**♦  NOTE:**
**In addition to my "master folder," I keep two others. In one, I put all the letters and cards I have received from friends and family; in the other, I keep copies of letters I have mailed.**

---

## Tell Others

Tell one or two people about your folder(s). Your spouse would be a natural choice. Another good choice would be to tell one or more of your children.

Whoever you tell should know where your folders, photo albums, journals, wills and other personal items mentioned in this book are located. If something happens to you (and trust me, it will one day), these people will be able to access the memories you have spent years saving and preserving.

---

**♦  EXERCISE:**
**Tell three people about your preservation folder and other important papers. Make sure at least one is not a relative and does not live in your household.**

---

## Family Bible

A family Bible can become a treasured memento to record the milestones in a family's history and to be passed on from generation to generation. This is also a great way to preserve key events in your family's life. Traditional dates recorded include births, marriages and deaths, although other information can be included. Many of the newer, larger family Bibles also have one or several pages devoted to a family's genealogy.

---

**♦ NOTE:**
**Family Bibles were much more popular in the 1800s and early 1900s than they are today. Two of the most treasured family history mementos my family has are family Bibles of my third- and second-great-grandfathers' families.**

---

Consider the following regarding your family Bible:

- Invest in a high-quality, full-size Bible. You are creating a treasure that, hopefully, will be passed on to many generations. Go first class.

- Make sure the Bible you purchase has a section inside for family tree information. Genealogy sections are usually found at the beginning or in the middle of a Bible.

- Once you've purchased your Bible, carefully record all information you are *positive* is accurate. Be sure to print neatly. (And please don't use pencil—it's hard to read and fades with time.) Whenever possible, record names, dates and places. Incorrect information entered at this initial recording can cause a lot of confusion in later years.

- Keep the Bible in a safe, accessible place. You will want to refer to your family bible often. However, because it is intended to last many generations, you will not want it to become too worn from constant handling.

- As events happen in the lives of your family members, add new information to the Bible. Deaths, weddings, births and baptisms are all events that should be noted. Space permitting, you may also want to include other family information.

■ Determine who in your family will be given the Bible when you no longer want to keep it. Make sure the recipient has a deep appreciation for, and interest in, continuing to update the family Bible.

---

**♦ NOTE:**
**Family Bibles make wonderful gifts for friends, family and your-self. My wife and I bought our Bible when our daughter was baptized. We dedicated the Bible to her, and, as our oldest child, will offer it to her one day to keep and preserve.**

---

## Family Heirlooms

A family heirloom is created when a family preserves and protects an item and passes it from generation to generation. An heirloom can be almost anything, such as the family Bible we just discussed or jewelry or handmade Christmas ornaments.

Heirlooms are important for several reasons. One, they offer a reward of enhanced family identity. Also, passing on family heirlooms allows future generations to see a record of your family's values and uniqueness. They are a part of you and your family's history, just like a video, journal or family portrait.

Consider the following regarding family heirlooms:

- Write down information about the item and its significance. Memories are short and fragile. Later generations will appreciate the heirloom even more if they have a clear understanding of its history and significance.

- It is unlikely one person will have all family heirlooms. Keep a master list of who has each family heirloom. This way an heirloom will not be "lost" when a relative moves away or dies.

- Display family heirlooms whenever possible. Family picnics and holiday gatherings are two great times to feature one or more heirlooms.

- At family events, encourage family members to bring the heirlooms they possess. Then take pictures and/or a video so more people can share the heirloom.

- Any items handmade by you or your relatives are especially valuable as heirlooms. Two examples include quilts and needlepoint.

- Take special care to preserve and protect your family's heirlooms (throughout this book preservation options and ideas are discussed).

- Educate younger family members about the importance of family heirlooms, as well as their responsibility to preserve, protect and pass on these treasures to later generations.

### Collections

Many people collect one thing or another, and these collections over time can turn into a family heirloom. Do you or anyone in your family collect something? Collections can be almost anything, including postcards, antiques, comic books, model cars, Barbie and G.I. Joe dolls, and baseball cards. Toys are another collector's item, and today many toys are aimed at collectors, not kids.

## Recipe Books

Most of us have childhood memories of foods we loved to eat and/or make. In particular, I remember my mother's marzetti and chocolate chip cookies.

These food memories should be preserved. One way to do this is to collect your family's favorite recipes and make a recipe book.

You can simply write down your recipes on 8 1/2" x 11" notebook paper, three-hole punch the sheets, and store them in a three-ring binder. To make copies for relatives, remove the sheets and have them copied. This is an easy way to make a small number of copies and to update your recipes.

An alternative is to have a book published based on your recipes.

Walter's Cookbooks in Waseca, Minnesota, will custom-produce your family's best recipes. You can publish up to 300 recipes, include photos and special messages, create a customized cover and add up to four pages of miscellaneous information pertaining to your family history. Prices vary depending on the number of cookbooks ordered; the minimum order is fifty books.

## For the Walls

### Frakturs

By definition, a *fraktur* is a German typeface that was developed several hundred years ago. Today, it is commonly used to refer to a lettered poster that describes an important event, such as a wedding or the birth of a child. You can buy an inscribed fraktur, add your family information, and then have the fraktur framed.

Frakturs aren't common. Check local craft and hobby stores, as well as magazines with a country living theme.

### Plaques and Trophies

Plaques and trophies can be a memorable way to preserve an important event or accomplishment. While mostly associated with sporting events, they can be used to commemorate any significant moment.

Contact your local sporting goods store or trophy shop for plaque and trophy information. The Erie Landmark Company in Chantilly, Virginia, is one organization that produces custom-letterered bronze markers for indoor or outdoor use.

## Wedding Gown and Other Clothing

Clothing can be an important family heirloom to preserve and treasure. The item kept most often is a wedding gown.

Have your wedding gown or other clothing item professionally dry cleaned and properly stored. Check with your local dry cleaner for information on services they provide. In Northern California, for example, a chain of cleaners offers a special wedding gown preservation service that includes inspecting the gown, cleaning it, repairing problem areas, pressing and packing. This service costs about $30—an investment well spent.

---

**♦ NOTE:**
**A gift certificate at a professional dry cleaner for a wedding gown preservation service is a nice gift for a newly married couple. This will help the young couple keep an important family heirloom for many years.**

---

Other items you might want to protect and preserve include a wedding tuxedo and certain children's clothing, such as a christening gown or a first pair of shoes.

## Personal Calendars

Many people keep calendars or other time management notebooks at work or at home. Consider keeping a separate calendar to record significant events that happened to you and your family during the year. I think of mine as my "best of the year" calendar.

Keeping personal calendars can be an exciting long-term project. Eventually, you will have your own library of yearly records.

When keeping your personal calendar, consider the following:

- Choose a calendar by a popular publisher. Remember, you are keeping a record that is intended to last for many years.

- Record family members' birthdays, including their date of birth.

- Record key events—both personal and work related. These can include trips, holidays, parties, work promotions and the like.

- List doctor and dentist appointments.

- Record books you have read.

Another option, of course, is to simply add personal information to your everyday calendar. For example, you could use different colored inks to differentiate work and personal items.

## Inventories

One way to make sure your family and friends know about your family history heirlooms is to make an inventory of important items. This can be as informal as notes written on notebook paper, or as structured as a computer-generated report that includes all important items in your home.

Note any of the following:

- Your "preserving the present" folder
- Frakturs
- Plaques and trophies
- Family tree charts and other written material, including journals, family histories and letters
- Wills
- Wedding gowns and other clothing
- Photo albums and special framed photographs

Be sure to list items given to you by your relatives that have a family history significance. These items include portraits, books, letters, Christmas tree ornaments—anything that has a value in your family's past.

When making an inventory of household items, check each of the following:

- Living and dining rooms
- Family room, den and office
- Kitchen and pantry
- Bedrooms
- Clothing
- Antiques and art
- Fine jewelry and furs
- Silver, pewter, and gold
- Fine crystal and fine china
- Cameras, video equipment and stereo equipment

Also check basements, attics, garages, yards and storage areas.

When taking your inventory, record the quantity, the date purchased and the original cost. If you can't remember how much you paid for an item, put down an estimate. For family history heirlooms, write a brief description of each item and note, if possible, the approximate date when it was produced.

You may want to take pictures of important items. Better yet, use a video camera, which allows you to verbally note special items and give descriptions about costs and other factors.

Once you gather the inventory and photographs, put them in a safe storage spot, such as your safe-deposit box at your bank.

---

**♦  NOTE:**
**For more information about inventories of your household items, contact your real estate or insurance agent. Also, many police departments or crime prevention units will visit your home and conduct an inventory of your residence and/or mark identification numbers on your personal property. During this time, they will also tell you how to make your home more safe and burglar-proof.**

---

## Important Numbers

Today most of us are innundated with numbers. It's a good idea to keep a record of your important numbers for your own use as well as for use by other family members.

Record and save the following numbers:

- Birthdate
- Social security
- Driver's license
- License plates
- Street address and zip code
- Telephone
- Credit card(s)
- Safe-deposit boxes (and location, too)
- Life insurance policies
- Bank accounts

## Time Capsules

The preservation ideas mentioned so far are relatively simple and inexpensive. In this section we will explore the time capsule, a more involved way of preserving the present. Preserving the present is like most hobbies; you can spend as little or as much money and time as you like. Time capsules require a greater financial and/or time investment on your part than the ideas prviously mentioned.

### Some Quick Tips

A time capsule can be fun for the people doing it and can be an invaluable (and even more fun!) resource for future generations. Think how interesting your descendants and relatives would find a treasure chest of items from your life. I know I would love to have found almost any kind of memento from my distant ancestors.

Why do people create time capsules? Paul Hudson, co-founder of the International Time Capsule Society (ITCS), says that time capsules reflect a desire to save something for the future. "Our lifetimes are so short, and this is a way that someone a hundred years from now, or even a thousand years from now, can see remnants of our lives. It's that urge for immortality we all have," Hudson states.

Located in Atlanta, Georgia, the ITCS maintains a registry of all known time capsules and serves as a clearinghouse for information about them. ITCS suggests the following for organizing your time capsule:

1.  Select a retrieval date. Options include sometime during your lifetime and many years into the future.

2.  Choose an "archivist" or director. Committees make decision-making difficult.

3.  Select a container. A safe is a good rule of choice. The interior should be cool, dry and dark. (See "Selecting the Container" in this chapter and "Organizations Mentioned in This Book" for companies that make time capsules.)

4.  Find a secure indoor location. Avoid burying your time capsule; they are too easy to lose.

5.  Select items for time storage. Try to have a mix of items, from the sublime to the trivial. The archivist should keep an inventory of all items sealed in the time capsule.

6. Have a solemn "sealing ceremony" where you formally christen the time capsule with a name. Invite the local media and keep a photographic record of your efforts, including the inside of your completed project.

7. Don't forget your time capsule! Try to "renew" the tradition of memory with anniversaries and reunions. Use your creativity at all times.

8. Inform the ITCS of your completed time capsule project. The ITCS will add your time capsule to its database in an attempt to register all known time capsules.

## Selecting the Container

Your time capsule can be simple or elaborate. This is one area in which you will want to consider making an adequate financial investment. You don't want the years and elements to ravage your hard saved treasures.

Think of the scope of your project when you select a container. Doing a time capsule for yourself, family, building, town or organization all require different levels of planning and storage dimensions.

The Erie Landmark Company (mentioned earlier) is one organization that produces time capsules of various sizes. Their custom options include walnut bases and bronze plaques for lettering. For other time capsule companies, see "Organizations Mentioned in This Book."

## Suggestions for Time Capsule Items

What should you include in your time capsule? Anything you want, especially those items that offer a glimpse of your life and the world you live in at the moment!

Some items should be unique or special, like a handwritten letter addressed to your great-grandchildren; others should be ordinary, everyday items, like stamps or current magazines. Items for your time capsule can include newspapers, magazines (especially fashion, sports and science), collectables (stamps or baseball cards), photographs, copies of important certificates or records, clothing, journals and a myriad of other possibilities. View your time capsule as your gift to the future. Be creative and have fun!

---

♦ **NOTE:**
**When creating a time capsule, think it out. Sadly, many time capsules are lost due to theft, secrecy or poor planning—people either forget their location or the fact that they exist at all!**

---

### Gifts to the Future

Creating a time capsule for a newborn boy or girl will be an incredible gift when it is opened in the future. See "Gifts to the Unborn or Just-born" in Chapter 7 for two companies that specialize in time capsules for newborns.

## Wills and Burial Plots

Thinking about your own death can be a uncomfortable experience. But let's face it: one day everyone—including you and I—will die. No mater how unpleasant preparing for your demise may be, it should be done *now* to ensure that your death and burial will be carried out to your exact wishes and wants. If you think about the legacies you are leaving behind, this can even be fun.

### Your Will

Every person over the age of 18 should have a legal will. Even if you do not possess a great deal, a will is one of the main ways you can:

- Control the distribution of your worldly possessions

- Describe your desires for burial and internment and gravestone or plaque

- Paint a picture of your life, using names, dates and places

The last point is something most people never do. In addition to noting the usual who gets what in your will, make your will a mini-narrative of your life and the lives of your immediate family. I'm not talking about a 15-page autobiography. I'm merely suggesting that you include a page or two of pertinent information, such as names, dates and places, relating to your life.

When consulting a lawyer regarding your will, ask if he or she experience including genealogical information. Contact your state's historical or genealogical society for help in locating a lawyer who is familiar with this practice.

The following shows family information that could be added to a legal will:

> My name is Timothy William Polk and I was born 21 February 1962 in Cleveland, Ohio. My parents were William Walter Polk and Sandra Lee (Evans) Polk. Toby Walter Polk, born 15 December 1968, and Tracy Lynn (Polk) Maxfield, born 13 January 1964, are my brother and sister.
>
> I graduated from Indian Valley High School in Gnadenhutten, Ohio, in 1980, and from The American University in Washington, D.C., in 1985.
>
> In November 1987 I moved to Sunnyvale, California. On 6 August 1988, I married Gyoconda A. Romero at the Church of the Resurrection in Sunnyvale. Our only child at this writing, Sandy Alexandra-Marie Polk, was born 3 May 1991.

Interested family members who later read your will will find a wealth of information about you and your family. Remember, your will should be safely stored in a county courthouse and be made available to anyone interested in reviewing it. Make it worth their time and energy to find it, and make it fun.

A final point: after your will is drawn up, tell several family members who your lawyer is and where your will is located.

## Giving Things Away

An important function of your will is to define the way you want your assests and personal property distributed. I would suggest you divide your material items into two parts, with one part being family history mementos and the other being regular assests.

The regular assests are all yours to decide and distribute. Here are a few thoughts to consider when you decide what to do with your family history and other life mementos:

- List all of your family history mementos (see "Inventories" in Chapter 2), and, of course, state who should receive each item. You may have formed a close relationship with a family member who shares your interest in preserving the past and present, and give *everything* to that person.

- List your written works (such as journals) and state who is to receive these.

- If you have a lot of items and no family to give them to, consider donating your paintings, furniture, books, etc. to your local historical society, museum, school or library.

- Consider giving your home to the The National Trust for Historic Preservation. This guarentees your home will be preserved and protected, and can lower your estate tax.

- You may want to make a financial donation to a preservation or other cause. The National Trust and The Civil War Trust (which is charged with preserving Civil War battlefields) are two to consider. If you have a large sum of money, you may want to donate funds to create a building, room or addition to your local school, church or library. Play your cards right (and donate enough money) and you could get your name etched in stone for years to come.

You do not have to die to give things away. A revocable living trust lets you do this. Very briefly, when using a revocable living trust, terms of the trust begin while you are still alive; you can change your mind as often as you want regarding who gets what. It is an excellent way to skip, or at least minimize, probate court (i.e., assets are released much quicker and your heirs may be able to avoid paying taxes to the IRS on the money). Consult your lawyer, of course, before you make any legal decision.

If you are over the age of 70, consider beginning to give family history mementos to your children and grandchildren while you are still alive. They will enjoy the receiving and you will enjoy the giving. Doing this while you are still alive avoids arguments and ensures that the items will not be "lost" after your death. Remember, you can't take it with you.

Giving during your lifetime can be exciting and rewarding. The National Trust, for example, has a program where you can donate your home to the Trust and still live in it. You will receive everything from peace-of-mind to income tax benefits.

---

♦ **EXERCISE:**
**Consider being an organ donor. What better gift could you give than the possibility of prolonging or enhancing someone else's life?**

---

## Your Burial

I know, I know. This is getting weird. But your burial is an important thing to think about and plan.

You must answer two main questions. The first is, do you want to be buried or have your body cremated? The second question to anwer is, where do you want your final remains to be stored or scattered? These are personal decisions that have a lot to do with your attitudes about life and death.

In the early to mid-1900's, the first was a relatively easy question to answer. People usually were born and died in the same town, and were buried in the town cemetery. Or they lived on a farm and were buried in a private family cemetery.

Times are different today. People move around more often and travel greater distances. As change accelerates more and more, the tugs of home are made lesser and lesser. The question of "where" becomes harder to answer.

I'm a perfect example. During the majority of my childhood, I lived in a small town in Southeast Ohio. For the past eight years I have lived more than 2,000 miles away in California; I consider it "home." In researching my family history, I discovered a beautiful cemetery in Dayton, Ohio, where three sets of my direct ancestors are buried. When my parents retired, they moved to Lexington, Kentucky. Where do I want to be buried?

If you are married, this should be a joint conversation. You and your spouse may want to visit some cemeteries to get a feel for their location and upkeep. Think about this. Think about the place you call home.

Another option, of course, is to have your ashes scattered at a place of your choosing. This can be done on a family farm; at the ocean where you used to sit and think; on a favorite golf course. The possibilities are endless.

Once you have decided on the destination of your final remains, consider how you want your burial or internment place marked. As anyone who has walked through a cemetery knows, gravestones can be very simple or very elaborate. Think about how simple or elaborate you want your marker to be. Decide what information you want it to contain. Consider what, if any, inscriptions to include.

Gravestone inscriptions can be fascinating. I enjoy walking through old cemeteries and reading the worn, weathered writings. One of my favorites is located in a cemetery in Cambridge, Massachusetts. In addition to the person's name and birth and death dates, the inscription reads:

*He graced, what few can grace,*
*a humble path.*
*This sod his body holds,*
*but God his spirit hath.*

You can write your gravestone inscription. Please do so—don't let others make that decision. Think about it now in a rational and relaxed frame of mind. Be creative, be classy and be imaginative. Remember, people will read your inscription for many years. Make your grave marker as memorable and as distinctive as your life.

---

◆  **WARNING:**
**Letting others create the inscription on your gravestone can be downright scary. How would you like to be immortalized with these words: "Those that knew him best deplored him most"? Or how about "Old and still"? Both of these, by the way, are actual inscriptions—I didn't make them up!**

---

## When a Relative Dies

When a relative dies who lives alone or who has no immediate family, you may want to volunteer to help sort through the person's belongings. Why? They will almost certainly have family history memorabilia that should be kept and preserved by your family. A stranger going through the items would not be as inclined or as informed as you to protect valuable family history heirlooms.

## Before Disaster Strikes

Anyone committed to preserving a part of their own and/or their family's life should take steps to safeguard treasured items from natural decay and natural disasters.

Fire, floods, hurricanes and tornados can destroy a home and its contents. In California, where I live, earthquakes pose another danger. In the earthquake of October, 1989, that registered 7.1 on the Richter scale, many people's homes were damaged beyond saving. Some people were never allowed to enter their damaged homes for even a few minutes; others were given fifteen minutes to go in and salvage what they could before their homes were declared uninhabitable.

Another recent California disaster, a forest fire, ravaged the drought-dried Oakland Hills area. Some unlucky people had fifteen minutes notice to take what they could from their homes before they were forced to flee the roaring inferno.

Time can be another enemy. You do not want your treasured writings to end up yellowed and brittle. Photographs should not be allowed to fade and be torn.

Take steps now to make sure your heirlooms are protected. This undertaking is well worth the investment.

### The 15-Minute Drill

Think of how panic-stricken you would be (at least I would be!) if someone had just told you that in fifteen minutes you could never enter your home again. Would you know what to do? Would you know what to take? This seems like something too improbable to happen, but planning for the worst is the best when it comes to preserving family heirlooms that cannot be replaced.

The first thing you should do is decide which items you would want to remove from your home in case of a natural emergency. Don't include stereos, TVs, furniture, golf clubs or other expensive items—they can all be replaced.

What you should include are items that can't be replaced. These include photo albums, video tapes of your family, journals, family history records, paintings, and any other items made, written, drawn or about your family.

Once you determine which items are "must keeps," take steps to store these items in close proximity and ready to be moved. A portable file cabinet, for example, is an excellent storage place for important papers and photographs. A safe is another storage alternative; while less portable than a file cabinet, a safe offers more protection and can withstand greater assaults from fire and other disasters.

♦ **EXERCISE:**
**List ten family-related items you would want to take with you to preserve if you were forced to abandon your home:**

1. _____
2. _____
3. _____
4. _____
5. _____
6. _____
7. _____
8. _____
9. _____
10. _____

Determine where in your house these items are located. Take the steps necessary to make them more mobile and more protected.

**Safety Deposit Box**

Some items are too valuable to leave at home. These should be stored in a safety deposit box at your local bank. Items you should store in your safety deposit box include:

- Stocks, bonds, savings bonds and other investment papers
- Photograph negatives
- Computer disks with important files
- Jewelery
- Passports
- Birth certificates
- Important family history documents

## Protecting Your Heirlooms

Make sure that the important family papers and heirlooms you spent time and energy collecting are properly cared for and protected. Remember, you are attempting to leave a picture of your life behind that, hopefully, will last for hundreds of years. Take steps *now* to clean, protect and preserve your gifts to the future.

What should you avoid? Dust, sunlight and heat are damaging. Water, dampness, humidity and even oil from your hands can wreak havoc with your heirlooms and papers.

What should you do? Store your items in sturdy storage boxes. Use acid-free papers, file folders and labels at all times. Invest in quality photo albums that use acid-free and PVC-free pages. Protect your photo negatives with a simple, efficient storage binder or album.

Don't expect to find these materials down the street in your drugstore. While some office supply stores are a good start, it is best to locate a company devoted to supplying preservation and protecting materials for museum-quality items.

The Preservation Emporium, of Dallas, Texas, specializes in "archival quality products for conversation, preservation and restoration of papers, photo-graphs, textiles and collectibles." I highly recommend you write or call for their catalog.

Another excellent resource for information on caring for materials stored in a person's home is available from the Kemper and Leila Williams Foundation in New Orleans, Louisiana. The Foundation publishes a 48-page phamplet entitled "Before Disaster Strikes," which sells for $6.95 plus shipping. "Before Disaster Strikes" describes how to prevent valuable materials from being lost during a natural disaster, as well as how to restore items already damaged. The foundation also offers a set of 16-page preservation guides on the following topics: family papers, photographs, paintings, furniture, books and matting and framing. The guides are $3.95 each, plus shipping.

Visit your local library or contact the National Trust for Historic Preservation to locate other preservation organizations.

## On the Road

When moving to a new location, take as many extra precautions as you can to protect your family heirlooms. Also, don't ship all of your treasures at one time. A woman I know lost everything when a truck carrying all of her belongings crashed and burned.

# CHAPTER 3

# Visual and Auditory Memories

*It is memories that link us to immortality.*
*As long as somebody remembers, you never die.*
*— Leo Buscaglia*

This chapter focuses on specific ways to record and preserve parts of your life through photographs, videos and audios. These topics are especially exciting to me because they are so new. Our grandparents, for example, did not have the opportunity to videotape the early parts of their lives. We live in an age when incredible technological advancements offer many more and better ways to preserve a part of the present than were available earlier.

## Photographs

After your preservation folder, photography is probably the next most important area to focus on to preserve parts of your life. Photographs can be invaluable tools in showing a "picture" of your life and recording a part of your history that is now past.

For all of us (and *especially* the family history addicts), nothing can be more valuable—and more frustrating—than photographs. They are wonderful when the people, places and events in the photo are identified; they are frustrating when the photos are unmarked and the people in the pictures are not known.

In this section, you'll learn about ways to preserve and enhance existing photos and about which pictures to take to capture the people and moments of your life. This section and the one following, "Video Possibilities," are closely related.

## Enhancing Exisiting Photos

Estimates from Kodak, the film manufacturer, indicate the average family takes approximately 840 pictures over seven years, at a cost of about $500. I'm guessing that the vast majority of those pictures are poorly marked (if they have any writing on the back at all) and are either stuffed in shoe boxes with the negatives or housed in low quality photo albums.

Your challenge is to accurately and safely label, store and preserve your priceless photographic memories.

## Three Steps to Success

Accurately labeling and storing photographs can be a challenging, time consuming endeavor. But, I am convinced it is time well spent and I know you—and in later years your relatives—will agree.

To get the most out of your photographs, follow this three-step plan:

1.  Select your best photographs.

2.  Label each photo accurately.

3.  Preserve the photos well in photo-safe photo albums.

When starting a photo project, consider the following:

■   Start with your most recent photos and work backwards chronologically. Don't try to do all of the photos at once.

■   Be selective with the photos you keep. You don't have to keep *all* the pictures you've taken. Select the best and/or the ones with the most variations of people, places and things.

■   Pay special attention to photographs of special occasions, such as weddings, birthdays, etc.

■   Be creative with cropping to get more pictures on each album page. Trim pictures that include too much sky, walls, etc.

Once you have selected your photos, it is *very* important that you label each. Trust me, you won't remember over time. And, in the event that you aren't around when someone else is trying to deciper your photos, the information in your memory will be lost.

When labeling each of your pictures, try to include the following information:

- The full name of each person shown
- The date and place the photograph was taken
- A short comment or two about the photo (for example, "Summer vacation 1993")

## Photo Albums

Once you label your photographs, it is important to store them safely. An ideal situation would be to put all (or most!) of your photographs in photo albums. This takes time, but the results are well worth it.

Be careful, though. Based on my discussions with photo experts, we have a photo album problem that is bordering on a national emergency. What is it? Basically this: the vast majority of the inexpensive photo albums in which many of us have saved our pictures over the last several decades contain harmful chemicals that eventually will destroy the pictures they are protecting. These include the magnetic albums where the plastic sheet lifts off, the photos are placed on the page and the sheet is replaced. The most damaging and widely used chemical culprit is Polyvinyl Chloride (PVC).

What can you do? Make sure you purchase and use photo-safe albums and adhesives. The best photo album pages use only polypropylene, which is sold under various brand names, including Mylar.

Contact you local camera or art supply store and inquire about their photosafe materials. Creative Memories, the Preservation Emporium, and Light Impressions are three companies that supply archivial quality products.

---

♦ **WARNING:**
**Even magnetic albums that claim to be "photosafe, no PVC" can be potentially damaging to your photos. Why? While the plastic protective sheet may be PVC-free, the paper and album glue may contain harmful chemicals that over time will harm photos. Make sure all parts of your albums are photo-safe—the plastic sheets, the paper and the glue.**

---

## Help is Available

If your photo project seems overwhelming, don't despair—help is available. Visit your local camera store and ask if they have information on preserving photographs or know of someone who does.

Creative Memories, mentioned earlier, is an organization that is dedicated to preserving photographic and other memories. Headquartered in St. Cloud, Minnesota, Creative Memories' more than 3,000 consultants give thousands of seminars each year on how you can safely preserve photographs.

## INTERVIEW: Preserving Photos with Paula Julianel

Paula Julianel is a Creative Memories consultant in Belmont, California. For the past four years she has held workshops on the care, preservation and safekeeping of family photographs. She also supplies her workshop participants with photosafe albums and supplies.

In this interview, Paula describes her mission and offers tips on preserving photographs.

QUESTION: *Tell us about your workshops.*

JULIANEL: *Our goal at Creative Memories is enrich the future and, of course, preserve the past. The workshops run between two and three hours. We start with getting a person's pictures out of the processing envelope and into an album. It's really hands-on, really fun. We also offer on-going support after the workshop is completed. We want people to not just start photo projects, but also keep those projects going.*

QUESTION: *How important are photo albums in preserving memories?*

JULIANEL: *Albums are very important. The "magnetic" albums that are so common are also so potentially damaging to a family's pictures. A whole generation of photos that are in magnetic albums will be destroyed. I hate to see so many people's memories destroyed in albums that are supposed to be protecting them. Why take a photograph if you're not going to enjoy it and preserve it?*

QUESTION: *What specific tips would you recommend to someone who is attempting to safely preserve their photos?*

JULIANEL: *Keep your photos in a cool, dry place. Attics and basements are terrible because they're either too hot or too damp and cool. Also, consider taking at least one roll of black and white film each year. Black and white pictures are more stable than color, as color photos will eventually fade no matter how they are protected. Also, you could attend a workshop.*

Creative Memories offers the following guidelines when selecting and using photo safe materials to protect your pictures:

- When writing on the backs of photos, use a felt pen with quick drying, permanent and fade-proof "pigma" or "pigment" ink. (Do not use a ballpoint pen, which will push through the front, or a felt pen, as they will smear or stick to other photos.)

- Use only "acid-free" and "lignin-free" paper for your albums. Paper should also be heavy enough (60 to 80 lb. weight) to prevent bleed-through from felt pens.

- Colored paper should be "acid-free" or "fade-proof."

- For albums, look for features like reinforced edges and cotton bookcloth coverings that will help your albums wear well over the years.

- Avoid plastics with PVC.

- Use adhesives for mounting photos that are made for photographs and labeled "archive quality" or "acid-free."

## Preserving Older Photographs

Hopefully, you have in your possession old photographs of your childhood or of your relatives. It is very important to label each photograph as discussed earlier in "Three Steps to Success." If you are not *exactly* sure about something in the photo, request help from a relative who would know for certain.

Damaged or faded photographs can be restored. Again, check your local camera store for more information. If they can't help you, they should be able to put you in touch with someone who can. A museum can be another resource for information.

Here are some ideas for utilizing old photographs:

- Create a family tree/family history photo album where each member of your family is shown one time.

- Make a composite family photograph on a chart.

- Create a photographic history of a person with photos of key events in their life.

- Add photographs to pedigree charts or family group sheets. (Family history buffs will know these terms; if you don't, contact a local genealogy society.)

---

♦ **NOTE:**
**Over time you may acquire numerous old photos in which you simply do not know who or what is shown or when the photo was taken. Don't discard these photos. Keep them to show an era that will never return.**

---

## Taking New Photographs: Family Portraits

In addition to organizing existing photographs, you will want to continually add new pictures. Taking a family portrait is one of the best ways.

Family portraits are not taken much anymore[2], and that's a shame. They create a wonderful snapshot of a point in time in a family's life. They are usually done professionally, and result in high-quality pictures. And everyone prepares for the photo session and thus looks their best (or at least tries!).

The challenge is being able to assemble all family members at one time. Special family events, such as weddings, anniversaries or holidays, are ideal times to take a family portrait, since everyone gathers in one location.

Family portraits do not have to be taken by a professional photographer or outside source. Large department stores, such as Sears and J.C. Penney's, are one less expensive alternative. If you have a friend who is an avid photographer, ask him or her to assist you with producing a family portrait. Many times someone in your family (even yourself!) will have a good camera that can take adequate, if not great, pictures. Just remember, if you are using a family member's camera, either have a friend take the shot or use a timer—you want everyone in the shot, including the person taking the picture.

How often should you take family portraits? It depends on your family and your interest. At least once every year is a good goal to shoot for. You might also try and take the picture at the same time each year. Two occasions that are especially appropriate are Christmas and family reunions.

---

◆ **EXERCISE:**
**When was the last time you were in a family portrait? Who was in the picture besides you?** _____

_____

_____

_____

---

[2] Or at least it seems to me.

## Taking New Photographs: Candid Shots

Candid shots offer an alternative to formal family portraits. These are the everyday pictures you and your family take yourself. They should be numerous, fun, inexpensive and show both special occasions and your everyday life.

If you do not have a camera, consider purchasing one. Cameras today are simple—you literally have to know how to load the film and then point and shoot—and relatively inexpensive.

Your local camera store will have a wide range of models and sizes to pick from. Go back several times and don't hesitate to ask questions. You will soon find a model that fits your needs.

When taking candid shots, remember:

- Capture people, places and things, such as your house and car.

- Try to catch the person's personality. If a person has a big laugh, take a picture when they are laughing. If they are known for falling asleep in a particular easy chair, take a picture when they are doing it.

- Show action shots, such as people cooking, barbecuing, playing games and sports.

- Take pictures during meals, particularly for special celebrations.

- Show a person's hobbies, both when they are doing what they do and, if appropriate, what they have collected.

- Be sure to include everyday shots, such as writing bills, doing laundry and washing dishes. These aren't glamorous shots, but they will give future generations a great look at how you lived your life at a particular time.

---

**♦ NOTE:**
**Make sure you have pictures of each member of your family. As a family history researcher, I can attest to the frustrating experience of finding information about a person's life, but not locating any photographs of them.**

---

## Copying Existing Photographs

You will probably discover photographs your relatives and friends have that you will want to copy. Ideally, they will lend you the photos and you can take them to a professional camera store to have copies made. If the photo is very valuable or very large, you may have to take a picture yourself and use that as the copy.

In addition to photographs, you may want to take pictures of other items including:

- Maps
- Illustrations in books
- Bibles
- Letters

---

**♦ NOTE:**
**Be sure and ask permission of the person or organization (such as a library) before you take pictures of existing photographs.**

---

## Negatives

Keeping all of your negatives is a smart thing to do, it's even smarter to keep them labeled and organized.

To label negatives, put them in 8 1/2" x 11" plastic negative sleeves and write with a permanent, fine point pen. These sleeves can then be put into three-ring binders for easy retrieval. As with photos, always use photo-safe, PVC-free storage materials.

At the very least, store your negatives separately from your pictures. In extreme cases where your photos might be lost or destroyed, your negatives will hopefully be saved to recreate your pictures. You will want to store very rare or valuable negatives in a different location, such as in a safety deposit box or at your work.

## The Value of Good Frames

Nothing enhances a good picture more than a high-quality frame. I would recommend, whenever possible, that you spend a little extra to get the best frame possible. Remember, you are attempting to leave something behind for several generations spanning several hundred (hopefully) years—do it right!

There are basically three ways to approach framing:

- Custom frames produced by a professional
- Semi-custom frames you make yourself
- Already-made frames purchased "off-the-shelf"

Your choices you make will depend on the amount of time and money you want to invest. If you have numerous photos, you may want to explore taking frame-making classes; over the long term you will undoubtedly save money.

When using custom-made frames for special photos, I like to include an area for text. To me, this enhances the picture; the short description identifies who and/or what is shown and approximately when the photograph was taken.

I included the following inscription with a picture I had framed for my Dad of himself, his father and the family dog Tanna:

> **Father, Son and Dog**
> **George Washington Polk, William Walter Polk and "Tanna"**
> This picture was probably taken during or shortly after George Polk's military service during World War II, which ran from 10 April 1944 until 2 February 1945. William "Bill" Polk was born 14 June 1937. He is about seven years old in this picture with his father.

Frames are available through many stores. One organization that has especially distinctive frames, as well as archivial-quality photo albums and storage boxes, is Exposures located in Oshkosh, Wisconsin. Write or call for their catalog.

---

♦ **NOTE:**
**Frames make great gifts, even if you don't include pictures!**

---

## Video Possibilities

Videotaping has tremendous potential for recording both the present and the past. I strongly recommend that you do whatever it takes to use video to capture a part of you and your family's life. Parents with young children, in particular, should use video—I can attest to the fact that kids grow up very quickly.

Today video cameras are becoming easy-to-use and affordable. You can purchase a good video camera for between $400 and $800; depending on your level of sophistication and the features you want your camera to have, you can, of course, spend much more.

Another avenue you may want to pursue is to occasionally rent video equipment. Rates often can be obtained for 24-hour or shorter rentals. Check your phone book or visit your local camera store.

### Special Events

Special occasions are a natural for video filming. Weddings, birthday parties, graduations and even births are wonderful moments that can be captured and the memories enhanced with a video camera. When filming at special events, think about these tips:

- Try to show as many different people as possible.

- Have someone say the date, place you are filming, and the occassion.

- Mix your filming with both action shots and formal poses.

- Have fun! The more enjoyment you get out of your filming, the more relaxed and spontaneous your video subjects will be.

### Everyday Occurrences

Just like photographing everyday events is advisable, so is videotaping these occurrences. Meals, gardening, washing the car—all of these and many more are of interest, because they show your everyday life and the time in which you are living. Concentrate on recording special occasions, but be sure and include everyday shots as well.

### Time Traveling: Part 1

A variation on recording current people, places and events for your family history is to make a video of your life's past. A friend of mine, Bob Will, has done this; he calls it "time traveling."

Bob brought his video camera to the town where he was born and had spent the first eleven years of his life. He had not been back in more than thirty years. He visited various places and filmed away, adding commentary when he felt like it and other times simply filming silently. Places he visited included his childhood home, a nearby field he used to play in, his grammar school and the church his family attended.

"I walked where I walked when I was growing up more than thirty years ago," Bob says. "I walked the area and photographed and listened and smelled and remembered the games, my friends, the picnics."

The feelings that came back to Bob were "great, very positive, nostalgic," he says. By capturing those sights and sounds on video, Bob says he can "recapture those feelings just by looking at the film."

The following are some places you may want to visit when creating your own personal history video:

- Homes you lived in
- Neighbors' houses
- Yards, fields, baseball diamonds or parks where you played
- Schools attended
- Churches attended
- Libraries visited
- Boy or Girl Scout camps and areas
- Town Hall and other local landmarks
- Fraternities or Sororities
- Any place you "hung out"

Feel free to include other places or things that jog memories. One of my still-fresh childhood memories is of a large buckeye tree located on the church grounds that we used to stop at in the fall on the way home from school. We would gather the prickly shells and crack them open to get the dark, smooth buckeyes that we would then play with and collect.

This can have many variations. If your family moved fairly often while growing up, record the various houses you lived in. Or focus on one or two places that had special significance to you, and spend in-depth time recording and exploring.

♦ **EXERCISE:**
**List ten places you would like to include in your personal history video.**

1. _____
2. _____
3. _____
4. _____
5. _____
6. _____
7. _____
8. _____
9. _____
10. _____

One interesting thing you may discover during this filming is that your perceptions and memories are different than the reality. "The long hallway I used to run down as a kid was about four adult steps," explains Bob.

Another exercise you may want to try is this: before you do your time traveling trip, think about and write down the earliest memory you have of anything. Then, during your filming, see if any particular place or thing triggers new, maybe even earlier, memories.

♦ **EXERCISE:**
**What is the earliest thing you can remember from your childhood?**

_____
_____
_____

**Today's date:** _____

## Time Traveling: Part 2

A second way to use video to record the past is to make a tape devoted to your family history. In this case, you will record those people, places and things that were or are part of your family. You might call this your family history video.

Obviously, you should include yourself and as many of your relatives as possible. In addition to people, you also can film houses, apartment buildings, schools, cemeteries, gravestones, churches and a myriad of other places and things that have special significance to your family.

To enhance the viewing, be sure and describe in detail what the viewer is seeing. You should include:

- The date you film
- What you film
- Where you are
- The significance to you or your family

♦ **EXERCISE:**
**List ten people you would like to interview for your family history video.**

1. _____
2. _____
3. _____
4. _____
5. _____
6. _____
7. _____
8. _____
9. _____
10. _____

---

♦ **NOTE:**
**When photographing or videotaping cemetery stones, you may**
**have to remove grass, dirt or other debris to see the stones fully.**
**Be very careful, as old headstones are particularly susceptible to**
**damage from the elements. Use a small broom and water to careful-**
**ly clean the stone. Never do anything destructive.**

---

### Time Traveling: Part 3

For this project, you'll travel to the future! Make a video every so often, say once a year, with your special message to the future. You might want to record this short message on the same date each year, such as on your birthday or on New Year's Day.

Have fun with this! Talk to your descendants. Tell them what your life is like at the time and your hopes, plans, goals and fears regarding the future. Take a tour of your house; show off any collections you have; note current world events, such as who is president; cook your favorite chocolate chip cookies. Leave something behind that the future will enjoy and treasure one day.

### A Video Heirloom

The three time traveling video projects just discussed focus on filming new video. There is another project you should strongly consider doing at least once that I call creating a video heirloom. What is this? A video heirloom is simply putting together existing video, photographs, and memorabilia, all spliced together and converted to VHS video suitable for playing in your VCR.

The final video can be extremely powerful and a gift family members will never forget. Think about the possibilities: splicing together old 8mm, 16mm and Super 8 video and new video, along with photographs old and new. Add music, captions and an introduction or summary and you can create a remarkable video story of your family's life.

Does "producing" a video sound daunting? Don't worry, there's help.

Mary Lou Peterson of Mary Lou Productions has produced a video entitled *Gift of Heritage* on how to create a video family history. It includes helpful information on getting started, organizing existing photos and video, and working with a video production company, among other topics.

To give the viewer a feel for what the finished product might look life, Mary Lou also includes parts of the heirloom video she produced about her family's history, and in particular her ancestors' immigration from Norway to the Midwest. *Gift of Heritage* costs $29.95, which includes postage and handling, and can be ordered from Mary Lou Productions.

> Mention you heard about Mary Lou Productions from this book and you'll receive a $2 discount when purchasing *Gift of Heritage*—I'm not kidding, you will!

### INTERVIEW: Creating a Video Heirloom

Once you decide to create a family video, you will need to find a video production company to assist with actually producing the video.

Show Video Gifts located near Buffalo, New York, is one such organization. Friends of ours produced a family history video with Show Video and I was amazed at the powerful and professional presentation.

John Gowan, owner of Show Video, says his organization has produced thousands of family video projects ranging from several minutes to several hours in length. In this interview, he describes the process and the possibilities when creating a video heirloom.

QUESTION: *Tell us about the video histories you and your customers produce.*

GOWAN: *People do a variety of things. We do a lot of* It's a Wonderful Life *videos at Christmas time. Many people just do short ones around a specific event, such as a cruise or baby's first year. I would say the average length is about 12 to 14 minutes. One person from Ohio had 2,000 slides that developed into more than two hours of video.*

QUESTION: *What tips would you suggest when starting a video history project?*

GOWAN: *I would say the main thing to think about is the order. How do you want to assemble it? Some people don't stay chronologically, and it still works. They take one person at a time and follow them throughout their life to that point, and then go back and do another person. I'd also recommend including memorabilia in addition to video and photographs, things like napkins and matchbook covers from weddings, ski lift tickets, whatever.*

QUESTION: *What's the biggest challenge when producing a great family life video?*

GOWAN: *The single biggest obstacle I see people having is procrastination. "I'll do it tomorrow," or "I'll do it for next Christmas." People want to do it, but everybody puts it off. I'll give you two examples of why it's important to do this now. One man had between 80 and 100 rolls of old film from his childhood. He kept procrastinating about converting it, and finally we began the project. Halfway through it, he learned he was dying of cancer. He turned it into a message to his kids: "By the time you see this I'll be gone..." type of thing. It was very emotional, very touching. Another example is when I kept after one of my friends to do a video, and he finally did it and it turned out beautifully. Two months after we finished, his dad died. He couldn't thank me enough for doing it while his dad was still living.*

> Mention you heard about Show Video Gifts from this book and you'll receive a free telephone consultation regarding your project, as well as free overnight shipping of your photographs and mementos during the production process.

## Possible Topics

Your video family heirloom can be many different things, both in length and subject matter focus. This is another example where your creative juices can flow. The following are possible topic ideas to base your video heirloom project on:

- A history of your life to date
- A history of your family's life to date
- A focus on one person or one couple's life
- A compilation of photographs and video from the past
- Special events, like weddings, graduations and vacations
- A Christmas tape chronologically showing the holiday over time
- A birthday tape, where a person's birthdays are shown chronologically

## Audio Recordings/Oral Histories

Audio recordings are similiar to video in their value to preserve part of a person's life. Not only do you learn about someone's life, a part of the person—their voice—is captured forever.

Audio is important for another reason; many people simply don't like to write. They won't leave behind letters, journals, diaries or any other type of written history. In these cases, creating an oral history by tape recording this person can be an invaluable way to record and preserve their life's most significant moments.

Everyone has a story to tell and they want to share their story. It's your job to ask and then to listen.

### Who to Interview

Hopefully, over time you will be able to interview all of your family members. Each will have a unique story to tell and will add a different perspective to your family as a whole.

I recommend starting with your oldest living relative and work backwards, from oldest to youngest. Also, put any relatives who are experiencing medical difficulties at the top of the list.

Don't forget to interview yourself. The next chapter discusses writing your autobiography. You certainly can, and should, do an oral autobiography, too.

### How to Interview

Your audio recordings can be simple or more formal, depending upon your electronic sophistication and your plans for the finished tape. You can, for example, add music, a narrator and special sound effects.

One way to enhance oral history recordings is to properly document the cassette, both on the outside label and on the tape itself. At a minimum, I recommend including the following information with each oral history cassette:

- Who is being interviewed.

- Who is asking the questions.

- The time and date (this could be over several days) the interviews took place.

- A brief summary of the person's relationship to you.

- The person's age at the time of the interview (include their birthdate).

Oral histories on audio are both valuable and fragile. Handle the tapes with great care. Remember these key points when you create an audio oral history:

- Use high-quality cassettes.

- Always have extra batteries and tapes available, should you run out.

- When finished, make multiple copies and send them to various family and friends. Keep a record of which tapes you have sent to whom.

- Keep all masters in a particular place. Depending on how much value you place on the tapes, you might want to keep them in a safety deposit box outside your home to protect against fire, flood, etc.).

## Conducting Interviews

Interviewing your relatives and friends doesn't have to be a painful experience for either the interviewer or interviewee. Your goal will be to create a record that includes factual information and also the person's thoughts and feelings about particular subjects. The interview should not be an inquisition. You aren't (or shouldn't be) trying to embarrass anyone.

Remember the following when interviewing a relative:

- Always ask the person's permission before taping. He or she must feel comfortable with what is about to take place. Explain, in simple terms, what you would like to do and why.

- Prepare the person before you interview them. You want spontaneous answers, but you don't want to surprise or embarrass the interviewee.

- High-tech equipment can be intimidating. Try to be as subtle as possible when you use video and audio equipment. For example, rest the video camera on your lap and tilt the viewfinder to the proper angle. Then, you can glance down occasionally to make sure your subject is still in the picture.

- People won't say things succinctly. Older people especially tend to ramble. This is great. Let them. What you are trying to do is capture them, not some polished answers to slick questions.

- Be careful when you interview relatives—their minds and their memories can play tricks. Try to verify what they tell you.

- Ask about the history the person has seen in addition to facts about their life. Most people have seen incredible changes take place in the world and in their lives.

- Ask about specific dates and places, and include questions to stimulate stories and personal observations. You don't want to create something that is simply a listing of names, dates and places; you also want to capture what the person is like and believes.

- Use photographs and other mementos to stimulate their memories.

- Keep it fun! The more relaxed a person is, the better and more spontaneous his or her responses will be.

The following are suggested questions to ask[3] when interviewing family members. These are appropriate for both video and audio interviews.

- What is your full name?

- What was the exact date and place you were born?

- What were (are) your parents names?

- Describe your parents. What were (are) they like?

- How did (do) your parents make a living?

- What were (are) your grandparents names? Describe them.

- Where did your family originate from?

- Did (do) you have any brothers or sisters? What were (are) their names and birthdates?

- What are some of your earliest childhood memories?

- What did you like to do most as a child?

- Did you have a favorite pet or toy?

- What schools did you attend?

- What were your favorite school subjects?

---

[3] Several of these questions are reprinted by permission from Bill Zimmerman, author of the book *How to Tape Instant Oral Biographies*. New York: Bantam Books, 1992.

- Name and describe your favorite teachers.
- How did you and your spouse meet?
- When and where were you married?
- Where did you honeymoon and what special times do you remember?
- Do you have kids? List each child's full name, birthdate and place of birth.
- How do you feel about being a parent?
- What are your favorite hobbies?
- What do you wish you could do more of?
- What do you think was the turning point in your life. Why?
- What has been the happiest time in your life? The saddest?
- Who was the first president you voted for?
- Where were you when JFK was shot?
- Who are your favorite authors? Movie stars? Professional athletes?
- What do you feel are your greatest accomplishments in life?
- What are your dreams?
- What special message would you like to leave for your descendants?

After the interview, thank the person and spend some time with them without the camera or tape rolling. Many times asking these types of questions stir up powerful memories and emotions for the interviewee.

## Other Ideas

### Build a Library

Hopefully, over time you will collect many video and oral memories worth saving. I strongly suggest you create a personal library of these tapes and label and store them properly. Never give away a master tape—always make and give away a copy.

### Distribute the Fun

Each time you tape a video or audio memory, consider sending copies to your relatives. They will certainly enjoy the information and the fun.

The down-side to this is the cost involved in purchasing tapes, copying from the master and mailing the tapes. To get around this, you might first send a post-card to your relatives describing your new tape and saying you will be happy to send them a copy if they first send you a few dollars.

# CHAPTER 4

# The Written Word

*If you would not be forgotten,*
*as soon as you're dead and rotten,*
*either write something worth reading,*
*or do things worth the writing.*
*—Benjamin Franklin*

Your writings can reveal and preserve a great deal about yourself and your life. Written projects also can be excellent gifts to those close to you.

This chapter may appear daunting to people who are afraid or dislike to write. Please give the ideas in this chapter a try. There are no wrong ways to write, only *your* way. A misspelled word is as much a part of you as a Shakespearean sonnet. No one is going to grade you; they are going to thank you.

I can speak from personal experience. Some of my most prized family history possessions are items written by, and to, my ancestors. For example, I have a letter written by my second-great-cousin from a hospital in Vicksburg, Mississippi, during the Civil War, dated July 28, 1862 (I believe the letter was dictated). The letter ends saying he is feeling better and hopes everyone at home is well. Harvey Evans, who wrote the letter, died the next day.

Another example is my third-great-grandfather Judge Stephen Evans. While serving as a member of the Ohio House of Representatives, one of his colleagues learned that his wife died and immediately began a 140 mile journey home.

In the Judge's letter to his own family, you can feel the despair and uncertainty he felt being so far away. "I have been looking for some time for a letter from you but I only received one since I have been here," the Judge writes. "I want you to write to me as soon as you receive these lines and let me know how you all are."

The signature
of Judge
Stephen Evans

The problem is that few people like to write. Whether we are talking about 100 years ago or today, people shy away from taking the time and effort to put their thoughts on paper. A friend of mine who likes to research her family history laments that her grandparents left almost no written records of their lives. "We are wishing every day (my grandparents) wrote more things down," she says.

In this chapter we will explore various written projects that are powerful ways to preserve a part of your life for future generations. And, as you will soon discover, an excellent side-benefit of writing is that you usually learn more about yourself during the process.

## Letters and Postcards

Letters are wonderful sources of information about a person's life. They're personal, inexpensive and distinctive—no two letters are exactly alike. Sending letters and cards is like sending someone a gift. As a family history researcher, I treasure the letters I have from my ancestors.

You, too, can be *one who writes*. It's simple; just do the following:

■ Write letters, postcards or notes to friends and relatives.

■ Keep copies of the letters you write for yourself.

If you're not a letter writer (and most people aren't), start out with short notes and work up to one-page letters. These letters don't have to be deep or complex or even be written for a particular reason. Write about the weather. Write about your job. Write about your family, your kids and where you're planning to go on vacation. Just write.

Before you send your letter, make a copy and put it in a special place—like your personal preservation folder. Most drug stores and post offices have copy machines that offer low-cost copies. You also may utilize copy shops or the library.

You also can send postcards. Postcards are wonderful because cards include other interesting information, namely the picture, the stamps and the postmarks.

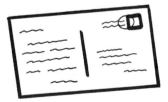

I like to send postcards to myself, too. Just jot down a few thoughts about the place you are visiting and send it to yourself. You will have a great memento of your trip, a snapshot of history (in the stamp, style of postcard, etc.), and you'll have a brief glimpse into your thoughts and actions at that time. Remember to date the postcard—the postmark isn't always readable.

---

♦ **EXERCISE:**
**The next time you are on a trip, buy at least five postcards. Send four to friends or family, and send one to yourself.**

---

The following are some tips regarding letter and postcard writing:

- Find time to stay in touch via the mail. Make time to stay in touch.

- Be sure to keep all the letters you have received from relatives. They're fun to reread every so often. And one day you can bundle together those sent by the same writer and give them to that person or to their kids.

- Enjoy the things associated with letter writing. Buy some nice stationary. Have a quality pen that makes writing fun. Purchase new and unique stamps.

- Don't wait to take a trip before sending a postcard. Purchase and send those showing your hometown, a local landmark or your state.

---

♦ **EXERCISE:**
**The next time you are in your local drug store or book store, buy at least five postcards depicting the town or area you live in. Send four to friends or family, and send one to yourself.**

---

## The Journal

One way to preserve a part of your life (and to experience personal enjoyment and growth at the same time) is to keep a journal. As the days add up to years, your entries paint a portrait of your life and your reactions to various events, people and places.

I can almost see some of you cringing. Please don't. A journal doesn't have to be a place where you wax eloquent on religion, politics and the state of your family. This is personal writing. You are writing for yourself. And, over time, these thoughts, jotted down even in a few paragraphs at a sitting, will add up to a treasure of insight into yourself and your life.

It is important to note that a journal is probably the one item discussed in this book that won't be read by others during your lifetime. Keep this private. Your thoughts are—or should be—of a personal nature and are not really meant for the outside world.

While you won't want others reading your journal while you are alive, you should let a few key people know you keep a journal and how they can obtain it later. In most cases, your journal will be several, if not many, volumes, probably in a variety of notebooks and other forms. You might mention your journal in your will.

### A Journal Story

Your journal can be many things, and one of the most valuable will be that it becomes an historical record. The following is an instance when my journal preserved an important part of my life.

I was a 16 or 17-year-old kid playing golf with my father and two others at River Greens Golf Course in West Lafayette, Ohio. On the seventh hole—a 135 yard par 3—my Dad had a hole-in-one. It was great fun, and has turned out to be the only hole-in-one either of us had, or even seen, to date.

As the years passed, we forgot the date of that round—Dad wasn't into preserving the present. One day, I was rereading one of my earliest journals and came across an entry I wrote the evening my dad got that hole-in-one. The date was June 21, 1978. I discovered the entry in May, 1993. For Father's Day in June, 1993, we bought Dad a wall plaque commemorating the fifteenth anniversary of his hole-in-one. Dad was thrilled and the mystery of the date of his hole-in-one was solved, thanks to my journal.

## Getting Started

To begin, determine what form your journal will take. Most people prefer writing in a notebook or blank book. These are inexpensive and allow you to doodle and add other material.

If your handwriting is hard to read, consider typing. Buy paper that is already three-hole punched and put each finished sheet into a binder. The disadvantage to using removable paper is the possibility, along with the temptation, that page(s) may get lost or may never get inserted. You also will lose some of the beauty of a handwritten journal.

Once you select your journal, simply start writing. I recommend you note at the beginning of each entry the date, the day of the week, and where you are at the moment. I also start the same way every time I write an entry; I tell where my wife and daughter are, briefly recap the major events of my day, then I move on to other topics.

## Some Journal How-To's

- Write on a regular basis. It doesn't matter if you write once a day or once a week or once a month, the important thing is to write. Don't wait for big events in your life. That's usually when you're too busy to write.

- Have a system, but be flexible. Are you taking a trip and don't want to haul around your large bound journal? Buy a special, smaller notebook to use during each of your trips. There are lots of forms a journal can take, including letters and logs—even writing letters to the future.

- Make sure your journal is ledgible. Nothing is more frustrating than finding something a person wrote and barely being able to make out the words. This is especially true with large pieces like a journal. Write slower than normal. Avoid using pencil, which tends to fade.

- If you use a computer, print a copy to paper frequently so nothing you write vanishes if your system malfunctions.

- Write what *you* want to write. It's difficult, but try not to think of others as you write. Be honest with yourself and write truly.

- Record events, but spend more time on what the events mean than on the events themselves. What is more important than the events are your feelings and your reactions to the events.

- Occasionally summarize what is going on in the world at the time you are writing. When rereading later, this can be an exciting historical record.

- Don't worry about following any rules. This is your book. It's impossible to go wrong.

## INTERVIEW: Journaling and You

Dr. George F. Simons has led journal workshops for more than a dozen years and has written three books on the subject. He holds a doctorate in psychology and theology from Claremont College and a diploma from the Gestalt Training Center of San Diego, California.

George says journal writing captures the essence of a person. "Truth is not only stranger than fiction, it is more compelling," he writes in *Keeping Your Personal Journal*.[4] In this interview, he offers tips and suggestions for journal writers.

QUESTION: *Would a journal be of interest to future generations who want to know about that person's life?*

SIMONS: *I, for one, am just fascinated with reading other people's journals. I really feel deprived that in so many cases (with my family) a journal doesn't exist. Photographs only go so far—what a person is saying, feeling, writing, all really bring them to life.*

QUESTION: *What advice can you give to people who have never had a journal and want to start now?*

SIMONS: *There are three key items in beginning a journal. The first is deciding what form your journal will take. The second is deciding what you will include in the journal. And thirdly, you'll want a pen that is nice to hold and fun to use."*

QUESTIONS: *How can a journal writer write for both him- or herself and posterity?*

SIMONS: *I try and face this question head on—this is for me. The key is to keep your journal private while you are alive. But there is no question about it: doing your own thing and having the guts to let others see it when you die is a challenge.*

QUESTION: *Are there any things a journal writer should avoid?*

SIMONS: *I would recommend not using computers. Even in reviewing a person's handwriting, there is art. But other than that, just try and remember that the journal is your own personal invitation to play.*

---

[4]Simons, George. *Keeping Your Personal Journal*. New York: Ballantine Books, 1978.

**To Get More Out of Your Journals**

In addition to preserving a part of your life, your journal can be an important growth tool. To get the most out of your journal, do the following:

- Occasionally reread your journals. Look for common themes that show what you spend your time on and/or what you focus on.

- Read your journal entries aloud, either to yourself or to family members. This will help you to get a better sense of your writing style.

- Record dreams and daydreams. Again, over time, patterns may emerge that you will find interesting and helpful.

- Use your journal to record your goals and plans for the future. Occasionally, jot down steps you are taking to accomplish your goals. Record those occasions when you reach or surpass one of your goals.

- Add newsclippings, drawings, photos, horoscopes, quotes you like, etc.

Remember, the journal is your own "personal invitation to play." Someday others may read it, but that is a long way off. Write for yourself and have fun.

## Other Journal-Related Ideas

For one reason or another, many people don't like or want to keep a journal. Whether you are a journal-keeper or not, I recommend you explore some of the journal-type projects that you can do without making the time or emotional commitments of a journal.

Blank books offer an excellent way to create lasting mementos of parts of your life. They are easy to use, inexpensive and often very beautiful.

---

**♦ NOTE:**
**You can find blank books in most bookstores and greeting card stores. One company that publishes high-quality blank books is Markings, a division of Thomas Nelson Publishers. Call or write for their free catalog.**

---

One way to use a blank book is to reserve it for special occasions and write in it only when that special occasion occurs. For example, you might keep a Christmas book and write one or two pages every Christmas day. Another good time might be New Year's Day. You could write about the past year and your plans and goals for the coming year.

My second-great-aunt, Mary Evans, kept a birthday journal. From 1867-1875, she wrote a small entry every year on November 23, her birthday. The entry was always the same, with of course her age being different. "This being my birth day (sic) I am sixty-four years old this day, " the entry would say. She would then sign her name.

This is a wonderful part of my great-aunt's life. It is fascinating to see the changes that take place in her handwriting as she ages from 64 years old to age 72 at her last entry. And it intrigues me about her life. I often wonder what compelled her to keep this birthday journal.

I keep a similar bound book that I write in every year on my birthday. In my case, however, I write a page or two, rather than the same sentence. The form you take is really up to you. Do whatever interests and feels right to you.

A variation of the same-time-every-year idea is to keep a bound book to give to your kids one day. For example, when your children are very young you may want to write a short entry every couple of months describing their development. You could also write a short note to your children on each of their birthdays. Think of the treasure you could give your children one day: an entire book that was written just for them over a period of years.

If you're a grandparent, write for your grandkids. Tell them what you've learned and would like to share with them. Show them, through stories and other anecdotes, what your life was like. Tell them about youself, so they will know more about themselves.

You also could write for your unborn child. This is especially powerful if you are a woman carrying a child destined to be your son or daughter.

Another idea is to keep a book on your hobby or favorite subject. Henry David Thoreau reportedly wrote 631 pages on wild seeds and had a 354-page manuscript on the dispersion of seeds; at his death, he left 3,000 pages of notes in twelve notebooks.

Other ideas you can record and preserve in blank books include prayers, recipes, and your child's early words, personal development (such as their first steps), well check-ups and sickness dates.

Another variation of the personal journal is to keep a family journal, in which all members of the family contribute. This could be one book where family members can write at various times and add other items, such as recipes and photos. A good location for your family journal is a common area in your house, such as the kitchen, the dining room table or even the bathroom!

---

**♦  NOTE:**
**Your project might even be suitable for a larger audience. H. Jackson Brown, Jr. wrote down bits of wisdom and advice for his son who was about to venture off to college. It was later published as *Life's Little Instruction Book* and became a run-away best seller. Brown's sequel, *Life's Little Instruction Book II*, also has sold millions of copies.**

---

## Your Autobiography

> *No matter who you are, where you were born,*
> *or where you live, you have a story to tell.*
> *—Fanny-Maude Evans.*

Writing your autobiography, as Fanny-Maude Evans says, is simply writing the story of your life. Each of us has a duty to tell our story for posterity. We must leave a legacy for the young. Each of our lives are different, each of our stories are different. Your autobiography, your story in your own words, can help others navigate their lives.

Writing your autobiography may be simple, but it is not easy. There is no question it will take time, commitment and a willingness on your part to record both the good and the bad of your life in a straightforward manner.

I strongly believe it is worth the time and effort. Your autobiography, however long or short, plain or fancy, would be an incredible piece of history about you and your family's life. And, just like with a journal, you are almost certain to learn something about yourself as well.

### Now or Later?

Do it now. If you're older (whatever that is), there is no better time than the present to write your autobiography. If you are younger, I recommend you write your autobiography up to the present; you can always update and add to it later.

---

♦ **NOTE:**
One of my favorite "Calvin and Hobbes" cartoons is about writing one's autobiography. Calvin is a young boy; Hobbes, his stuffed tiger, comes to life when no adults are around. Hobbes walks into the room and sees Calvin writing. "Whatcha doing?" Hobbes asks. "I'm writing my autobiography," Calvin replies. "But you're just six years old," says Hobbes. "I've only got one sheet of paper," Calvin replies.

---

## Getting Started

Before you begin writing your autobiography, you may want to learn a little about the autobiographical genre. Fanny-Maude Evans' *Changing Memories Into Memoirs* is an excellent how-to resource. Reading a few autobiographies might also help. Two that are considered very good are Malcom X's *The Autobiography of Malcom X* and Virginia Woolf's *Moments of Being*. Read some current autobiographies, too.

You also can take a college or continuing education course on biography/ autobiography. Participants in these classes are usually asked to read certain autobiographical works, to write part of their autobiographies, and to discuss their writing with fellow classmates. Check local college and community continuing education programs for these classes.

When you're ready to start, write an outline of what you want to cover in your autobiography. You will want to emphasize the turning points in your life—both good and bad. Many autobiographers write about the bond between the past and present. The "why?" "where?" and "because" of your life today is often a result of your past. Remember, you are unique. Tell your story and your uniqueness as a person will come out. Only you can tell it like it really was.

From a preserving perspective, you will want to include some key elements. Important dates are valuable information, as are places where you lived. Record the unpleasant, too. Don't, for example, skip over your marriage that ended in divorce. People reading your autobiography in later years, especially those ancestors with a deep interest in your life, will want to know at least some of the details of your unpleasant memories.

A simple way to include this type of information is to devote one chapter solely to important dates and events in your life. This would be like a time line. Later, in other chapters, you can expand on the key areas that you want to tell others about.

Events you will want to note should include birth dates of you and other family members, moves to new houses, important school dates, college life, college graduation, your first job, marriage(s), birth of children, promotions, moves, etc.

---

◆ **EXERCISE:**
**List ten of the most important events in your life that you would**
**want to expand on when you write your autobiography.**

1. _____
2. _____
3. _____
4. _____
5. _____
6. _____
7. _____
8. _____
9. _____
10. _____

---

## Some How-To's

Following are some things to consider when writing your autobiography:

- Interest the reader early with a striking, life-changing story. Make the reader care early in the work.

- Write what you want to write. Don't write for others.

- Be sure to include full dates of key events, like births, marriages, etc.

- Note the places where events happened, in addition to the dates.

- The first time you introduce a relative, give his or her full name and relationship to you.

- Be honest; write from the heart.

- Write about the good *and* the bad, the highs *and* lows.

- Add visuals if possible, even if they are relatively crude. Put in maps, timelines, your family tree chart, etc. Sketch a layout of your hometown.

- Write what you *feel*. Facts and events are important, but what is most interesting is how you reacted to the various events. Events are secondary to the emotions they produce.

- Ask your kids what they want to know about your life.

- Write everything you can, then later edit out unwanted material.

Don't worry how "good" you write. You're leaving a part of yourself behind, not trying to land on a best-seller list.

## Overcoming Writer's Block . . . Getting Started, Part 2

Use the following ideas as starting points for sections in your autobiography:

- Write about your "birth myth." Your birth myth is the story surrounding your birth. It is a "myth" because you were too young to remember any of it. You only know what you were told.

- Was school important to you? Did you enjoy it? Was there a teacher who influenced you, either positively or negatively?

- What are your most vivid memories of childhood? Many autobiographers spend a great deal of time writing about their childhood—many critics call this a yearning to return to a simpler, more pleasant time.

- Write about your hobbies. If you could pick your ideal job, what would you do? How would you spend your ideal day?

- Who is (was) your hero?

- What famous people have you known or seen in person? For example, I have seen two U.S. Presidents (Ford and Reagan) in person, and I once shared an elevator with actress Linda Carter (we looked at each other eye-to-eye, and I'm 6 feet 4 inches tall).

- Think about the history you have seen and experienced. Living in the 1990s, many of us are witnessing the greatest changes in the history of the world. Think of the changes my grandmother, Dorothy (Furay) Evans, who was born in 1903, has seen in her lifetime!

- Mementos bring back memories. Do you have some "things" that hold special memories? Which objects and memories are special for you?

## A Note of Caution

It's common to have trouble writing about people who are still alive. Try it, but if it's too painful or makes you too uncomfortable, leave these parts out. This is your autobiography. You can include or leave out anything you want.

## INTERVIEW: The Autobiography . . . Spilling Your Guts

Marilyn Yalom is a Senior Scholar at the Institute for Research on Women and Gender at Standdford University. She is a specialist in French and comparitive literature, and edited, with Susan Bell, the book *Revealing Lives: Autobiography, Biography, and Gender.*

Marilyn has studied the autobiography extensively. In this interview, she offers suggestions on ways to enhance an autobiography.

QUESTION: *What is a good way to begin writing your autobiography?*

YALOM: *Writing down significant events and then expanding on them is a good way to begin. After you've written down several, you can later tie them together in whatever way seems appropriate.*

QUESTION: *What should a person focus on when writing their autobiography, to paint a portrait of their life for future generations?*

YALOM: *You must always be asking yourself, "What am I writing for? Who is my audience? Is it myself? My family? Or will this be published for a larger audience?" You have to make it interesting, too, regardless of who is the final audience. Ask yourself, "Does the reader want to read this? Will the reader learn something about my life?" Keep those questions in mind.*

QUESTION: *I heard you say once an autobiographer must "spill your guts." What do you mean by that?*

YALOM: *Did I say that? It doesn't sound like me! Anyway, I believe the point I was trying to make is that autobiographies should have emotional depth to them. It really is a form of self exploration.*

QUESTION: *What advice can you give autobiographers struggling to write about people who are still living?*

YALOM: *It can be a problem. Use disgression and try and put yourself in the other person's shoes. The line between telling your story and telling someone else's story can be very fuzzy. Use extreme sensitivity.*

◆ **EXERCISE:**
Use the following as a starter outline for your autobiography. Map out seven key areas you want to write about. Your birth, childhood, school, marriage and family will probably appear. What areas do you want to concentrate on? Try to record the key turning points in your life, both positive and negative.

The Autobiography of: _____

Date: _____

Outline:

I.


II.


III.


IV.


V.


VI.


VII.

## A Written Family History

Writing your family's history can be one of the most rewarding projects you will ever undertake. You will be able to give to your family a gift that is both priceless and timeless. And I guarantee you will learn more about yourself when you write about your ancestor's lives.

The key to writing a family history is information. If you have information that either you or a family member has gathered, you are ahead of the game. If you're new to the family research game, I recommend you read Chapter 8, "Family Research Basics," before you read this section.

### What to Include

Strive to include any information you have about yourself, your relatives and your ancestors. More is always better than less when writing about a family member.

I broke my family history project into four sections—one for each of my grandparents. Then I worked backwards, starting with the oldest ancestor I had information on in each section. Many times, I only knew a person's name and a few important dates in their life—usually their date of birth and death, although sometimes I also had a marriage date. With others, I found information on where they went to school, their military service and their jobs.

Include whatever personal information you have available about the person. Just be sure to identify where the information came from. I use a great deal of oral history; I just make sure I say it is oral history and not provable fact. For example, several people have told me that my great-grandmother Rachel Evans liked and kept canaries. I put this in my family history and labeled it oral history, because I have no proof that Rachel's penchant for canaries is true.

Once you have written all you know about your ancestors, add a section on yourself. If you haven't written an autobiography, this is a good place to include autobiographical information. I also recommend including a section that describes your family history project. What compelled you to start? How long did you work on it and when did you complete it? What was your life and the world like at the time you finished?

---

♦ **NOTE:**
**If reading about families interests you, there are several good books worth exploring, including *Roots* by Alex Haley, *Buddenbrooks* by Thomas Mann, and *Angle of Repose* and *The Big Rock Candy Mountain* by Wallace Stegner.**

---

### Getting Started

A family history can be a huge project. Consider focusing first on one or several periods in your family's life and writing about those. For example, write about the four-day time span when President Kennedy was killed and then laid to rest. Describe a relative's wedding (or yours). Write about moving to a new town, in a new state.

Begin by using short time frames or segments. You can link them together later.

### Keep It Simple and True

Keep you family history as simple and as truthful as possible. Be careful not to embellish or to "selectively forget" key elements. Include the positive times as well as the not-so-happy moments.

### Don't Be Discouraged by Your Family's Response

One woman I know spent several weeks huddled in front of a Macintosh computer writing about the time her family was forced to flee the Nazis during World War II. When she was finished, she had more than fifty pages of family history.

The woman made copies which she gave to her husband and to her two grown children. For several weeks, her husband was "too busy" to read it, which hurt the writer's feelings. One day, the husband unexpectedly found his wife and gave her a hug and a kiss, and thanked her for her story—it had moved him deeply and since then they have developed a new closeness.

Some members of your family won't be particularly interested in your family history writings. Don't despair. Many others will, both now and in the distant future. Write the best family history you can, the one you would want to read, and let others accept it on their own terms, in their own time.

## Final Thoughts

You must make the written projects mentioned in this chapter available to family and friends, or your efforts will do little to preserve the present. This is where publishing and distributing your written work becomes important.

### Publishing

You can be as fancy or as plain as you want to be when you publish your written projects. It's fine to handwrite your projects, as long as your handwriting is readable by others. A simple way to test this is to give someone a sample of something you have written and get their feedback on how ledgible your writing is. The last thing you want to do is write pages and pages that no one can read.

Many people feel comfortable typing. This is a good way to keep things neat and organized. If you have access to a computer and are proficient using desktop publishing software, I highly recommend you do so, because it is so easy to update information. When publishing this book, for example, I did all the work on a computer. I used a word processing package when typing the manuscript, then dropped the text into a page layout program. I did all typesetting and design—other than the cover—via the page layout program.

Once you have the content in a presentable form, decide what publishing route to take. One way is to take a master of the project to a copy shop and make a limited number of copies for family and friends. This is probably the easiest and cheapest way to proceed. You can then buy notebooks and insert the pages for safekeeping.

You can also have your family history professionally bound and published. Some printers specialize in "short runs" for just such a project. You will spend more money than at a copy shop, but the final product will be more professional and "finished." Check the *Yellow Pages* or your local library to locate these specialty printers.

---

♦ **NOTE:**
**Always, always, make copies for yourself of any writing projects. This is especially true during the publishing process.**

---

## Distribution

As I've said before, it is absolutely critical to distribute your written projects once they are in a published format.

Here are some distribution ideas:

- Give copies of everything to at least one person who knows about each of your written projects. As a young writer, Ernest Hemingway and/or his wife lost an entire suitcase of the "Great One's" stories—all of which were originals that had never been copied. (In those days, writers used carbon paper, and kept the carbons separate; in Hemingway's case, he had both the originals and the carbons in the same suitcase.)

- Give your written projects as gifts. This might sound a little corny, but people will appreciate your homemade projects, much like they did when you were a child and gave them hand-made gifts.

- Splurge a little. If you spent the time to write and publish a family history, for example, send a copy to *all* of your family members.

- Send copies of appropriate projects to local libraries and historical societies. Someday, someone doing family tree research will stumble upon your project. In his or her mind, discovering your project will be like finding a gold nugget.

## Summing Up

Don't miss the opportunity to put things on paper about your life and that of your family's. The personal history you know and any information you have or have been told will be useless to others if it's not passed on. Even handwriting can tell a lot about a person.

Write about anything that gets you excited, that *moves* you. Write.

# PART 3

## Making Your Mark

# CHAPTER 5

# A Life Worth Preserving

*I chatter, chatter as I flow*
*To join the brimming river,*
*For men may come and men may go*
*But I go on for ever.*
—*Alfred, Lord Tennyson, The Brook's Song*

Up to now, ideas have been presented about ways to preserve parts of your life for present and future generations. Chapters 5 through 7 focus on ways to lead a better, more meaningful life. The premise is a simple one—you will be more apt to strengthen your family ties and preserve a part of your life if there are positive things to remember and record about your life.

We are really talking about perpetuating your life—a form of immortality, if you will. By making a positive difference in this world, creating something that outlives your physical presence, you will not be forgotten. You will have achieved a form of immortality. That's really the definition of perpetuate—to preserve from being forgotten.

Recognize that building a better life, one that is worth preserving, is relatively simple. It's not *easy*, however, and that is where the challenge comes in.

Good luck!

## The Search for Meaning

At one time or another many of us are troubled by nagging thoughts about whether or not our life has meaning. We ask questions such as:

*Why am I really here?*
*Where am I going?*
*Will what I'm doing with my life make any difference, now or in the long run?*
*Is the world a better place because I got out of bed today?*

Humans have a basic need: we need our lives to have enduring meaning. The search for meaning involves coming to grips with what it is to be a human being who lives, loves, works, plays, suffers and dies. It can be a difficult, soul-searching undertaking.

One Holocaust survivor summed up his quest for meaning in life this way: "I want to be able to think I did something with my life that eventually, when I die, I will be proud of."

The fear of death plays a large role in this quest. In her book *Finding Your Purpose*,[5] Barbara Braham writes, "None of us wants to think that we have lived and died without leaving any trace of our uniqueness behind."

Realizing the need for your life to have meaning is an important first step in your search for a meaningful life.

*The meaning of life is not something*
*you understand—it's something you live.*
*—Harold Kushner*

## It's Up to You

Once you recognize your desire to create a meaningful life, the next thing to note is that achieving this is dependent upon only one person in this world: you. As a human being, you are responsible for your own life. You have the ability to take whatever action you desire; you can be proactive, rather than reactive.

One of the most exciting aspects of this capability to act is that you have the ability to improve the quality of your life. And, perhaps more importantly, you have the ability to positively touch the lives of hundreds, if not thousands, of others.

[5]Braham, Barbara. *Finding Your Purpose*. Menlo Park, CA: Crisp Publications, 1991.

## Your Personal Mission

Probably one of the greatest fears most of us share, in one form or another, is to be close to dying one day and to realize that we haven't done what we wanted to do with our lives.

To combat this fear, each of us needs a purpose in life, a mission, something we are passionate about and guides our life's actions.

A personal mission statement provides the overall guiding direction in which you move. It's a short statement that outlines how you will achieve your vision in life. It expresses what you do, the purpose for which you exist.

Your role in this world is unique. No one else has your combination of values, interests and abilities. The key is discovering and embracing what your mission is.

A personal mission statement might be: "My mission is to live with integrity and to make a difference in the lives of others." Another might be, "My mission in life is to live as ecologically soundly as possibly, while being a successful spouse, parent and business person."

---

♦  **EXERCISE:**
**Write down your personal mission statement. Be sure and date it.**

_____

_____

_____

_____

**Today's Date:** _____

---

Your personal mission statement should be the impetus that propells you toward your mission. Don't look at it as something you have to do, something that limits your enjoyment or passion in life; a mission should enhance your life.

## Your Personal Vision

Your personal vision is your mental image of what you want to be, create and do in the future. While your mission is the guiding direction, the vision is where you ultimately want to end up.

How bold should your vision be? In my opinion, the clearer and bolder your personal vision, the better. Think big when crafting your vision. Make it huge, grand and exciting. Remember the moon-shot, when President Kennedy challenged the U.S. space community to put a man on the moon? Impossible? No. Think of the Japanese and their practice of creating business plans that stretch 100 years or more into the future. Ridiculous? Hardly. Noted author and consultant Dr. Cynthia Scott[6] put it perfectly during a workshop about visioning when she said, "Little visions are not worth committing ten years of your life to create."

---

◆ **NOTE:**
**Are you comfortable with your life right now? Are you *too* comfortable? Don't lower your standards. Don't except less than all you can contribute to this world. Good enough isn't.**

---

If you don't have a personal vision, something you are moving toward with certainty, create one now. Don't worry about how outlandish or improbable it may seem. This is your opportunity to live your life in the exact manner you desire. Think to yourself, "What would I do if I knew I couldn't fail, that no forces could stop me because of my persistence and passion? What would I do?"

As you create your personal vision, remember that it should be something you care deeply about and is compatible with your deepest-held values and beliefs. In other words, it should be right with both your head *and* your heart. Your personal vision should be so clear and so exciting that it makes you want to get out of bed on a cold, rainy day.

---

[6]Cynthia Scott, care of: HeartWork, Inc., 461 Second Street, Ste. 232, San Francisco, CA 94107-1416.

---

♦ **EXERCISE:**
**In the space below answer these questions: What is it that I *really* want in my life? What am I passionate about in my life?"**

_____

_____

_____

_____

_____

---

## Personal Goals

Setting personal goals is another component in creating a meaningful life.

How do goals fit in with the mission and vision? While the mission and vision tend to focus on the "big picture," goals are specific actions to achieve specific results. They are the action steps needed to achieve your personal mission and vision.

To get the most out of your goals, link them to your mission and vision, write them down, make them specific, include a time element for completion, and make them measurable. Your goals should be challenging yet realistic. These are things you can do, actions you can take, to enhance your life. Make them big but reachable.

Set both short-term and long-term goals. Short term goals include:

- Visit five European capitals by the year 2000

- Contribute x number of hours a year to a volunteer cause

- Plant and grow an organic garden

The following are examples of goals to achieve over the course of a lifetime:

- Have a child

- Plant a tree

- Write a book

♦ **EXERCISE:**
Think about your personal mission and vision, and then write down three short-term and three long-term goals you would like to accomplish during your lifetime.

**Short-term**
1.

_____

2.

_____

3.

_____


**Long-term**
1.

_____

2.

_____

3.

_____

## Making a Difference

There are untold ways to make a positive difference in this world—to "make your mark," if you will. The ideas that are presented throughout most of this book can make a difference in your family life. Following are some ideas that hopefully will ignite an idea or spark an interest with you for making a difference *outside* your family life.

Gary R. Collins, author of *You Can Make a Difference*, calls people who take positive action "difference-makers." Be a difference-maker.

---

◆ **NOTE:**
**"Making your mark" is this: making a significant achievement that will be remembered by yourself and others for a long time.**

---

### Community Service

Giving something back to the community where you live can be a rewarding endeavor. The key is to get involved with something that interests you—your passion will propel you to do much more than if you join a cause just to join.

Libraries are one institution currently ravaged by budget cuts. Why not volunteer at your local library? Attend Board Meetings or join your library's "Friends of the Library" group. If one doesn't exist, start one! Brainstorm with yourself and others about how to enhance the library. Don't set any limits. Add a room? Recruit other volunteers? Add a wing? Tear the thing down and start over, from scratch?

Schools are another area begging for assistance from the community. Run for the school board, assist a teacher one day a week, volunteer to be an assistant coach for a sports team, lead a fund-raising drive. Probably nowhere else in your community will you be able to touch more young lives than by getting actively involved with a school.

Other groups continually seeking volunteers include local youth programs, the United Way, your church, Big Brothers and Big Sisters, and the Boy Scouts and Girl Scouts, to name just a few. See Chapter 7 "Giving Gifts That Last a Lifetime" and "Organizations Mentioned in This Book" for other organizations.

## Mentoring

Giving something back as a mentor to another person can be a rewarding experience. As you help others to change and grow, your life will also transform. Many mentors who give of their time and advice without expecting anything in return also have that—the idea of giving freely—carry over into other parts of their life.

What is a mentor? He or she is a tutor, a coach, a helper. Mentors are sounding boards for new ideas. As the mentor and mentee work together, the mentor's experience and skills are passed on to the mentee.

---

**♦ EXERCISE:**
**Almost everyone has had a mentor in one form or another in their life. Who has made a difference in your life?**

_____

**Describe how this person has helped you.**

_____
_____
_____
_____

---

Examples of mentoring can include, but are not limited to:

- Giving advice
- Offering encouragement
- Listening to problems
- Helping to set goals/inspiring
- Introducing the mentee to key social and business contacts
- Coaching particular skills or talents

The mentoring process can be a single action or a long-term plan. Do what feels right between the two of you. Don't worry if it is not structured; many of the best mentoring relationships are informal and on-going.

**Preservation Causes**

It's important to save both the present and the past.

If you are interested in preserving the past, I urge you to join the National Trust for Historic Preservation. Located in Washington, D.C., the Trust was chartered by Congress to encourage public participation in the preservation of sites, buildings and objects significant to American history. The Civil War Trust and the Association for the Preservation of Civil War Sites are two national organizations dedicated to saving and preserving Civil War sites.

You can also contribute to preserving the past by joining a local historical or genealogical society.

**Summary**

Most people will probably never be difference-makers on the scale of a Roosevelt, an Eisenhower, a Gandhi, a Mother Teresa. But to the best of your abilities you can make positive changes in this world.

The key is to take action. Many people know what to do; they just don't carry through. Find a cause and help. Find a need a fill it. Lose yourself in something bigger than your life, something that challenges you and makes you stretch. Find a reason for making a difference.

And take action. Stand up and be counted; don't sit on the sidelines. As the famous athletic shoe advertisement says, "Just do it."

Make your mark in your family's life and the world.

---

# CHAPTER 6

# The High-Touch Family

*Relationships and togetherness must be lived in the present.
You have to live now. You have to enjoy it now.*
—Leo Buscaglia

Strong family relationships can enhance your present life and can be an important legacy to leave behind for future generations. This chapter touches on several ways to strengthen family bonds, no matter how scattered about family members live.

## Families in Touch

Families are becoming more spread out and more diffused. This makes it increasing important to stay in contact and to keep the family bonds intact.

The following are several ways for families to keep in contact and remain close.

### The Family Newsletter

A family newsletter is a great way to communicate regularly with friends and family. It's personal, fairly easy to produce, and is usually cost-effective.

As with most things, your newsletter can be as fancy or as simple as you prefer. I mail an occassional letter to family members that is simple and inexpensive. I include news regarding my young daughter's progress, items I've recently discovered that relate to our family history, and any news bits supplied by other relatives. I type the text on a computer and follow a newsletter format. The letter consists of a standard 8 1/2" x 11" paper, printed on both the front and back. I use mini-headlines to break up the topics. The result is something personal, yet easy to reproduce and mail.

My friend Michele Smith communicates with a group of about thirty friends and family via a newsletter she sends every other month. It details her latest adventures and the high points in her life during the previous sixty days. Michele also includes either drawings or a picture of herself, usually with several of her friends.

Is Michele's letter fancy? No. It's hand-written and photocopied. The pictures usually turn out quite dark, but still discernable. Each time, Michele uses a different color paper. Some colors are pretty and easy on the eye; others are bold and attention-getting. Michele usually leaves the bottom quarter on the back page blank so she can write a personal note to each person.

Her newsletter isn't fancy but it's unmistakably Michele.

## INTERVIEW: A Family Newsletter with Michele Smith

QUESTION: *How long have you been doing your newsletter, and how did the idea first come about?*

SMITH: *I started my newsletter (about three years ago). I used to do it monthly, but now I do it bi-monthly. My purpose was simply to keep in touch with people who are special to me. I have relatives and friends who live everywhere. Rather than writing the same thing many times, I just write it once. I also leave room at the bottom to write a short, personalized note.*

QUESTION: *How do your friends and family react to the newsletter?*

SMITH: *A lot more people write back to me than before! Some friends and family I only used to hear from once a year, at Christmas. But this helps us keep in touch throughout the year, not just at the end. I've also found that people who receive it pass it on to other relatives and friends who don't. My relatives back East, who I don't speak with all that often, called last week and said we all got together and talked about what Michele has been doing.*

QUESTION: *What satisfaction do you receive from writing and sending your newsletter?*

SMITH: *This is my way of keeping organized. Every two months I go through any new photos I have and the letters I've received. The newsletter is just the written extension of that. It's fun to answer the question, "What have I done in the last two months?"*

QUESTION: *What tips can you offer to others?*

SMITH: *I'd say the big thing is to make it interesting for people. I use different colored paper each time, and that's why my mom says she reads it. Keep your writing brief and concise and highlight the fun and interesting. Don't make it a mundane list of things that happened to you, such as your car broke down. Make it fun.*

Following are some ideas about producing a family newsletter:

- Get as many people to participate as possible. Try to get "contributors" who will pass along information they know. One person can't do it all.

- Honor a different living relative with each newsletter. Include humorous or moving anecdotes, and tell them "thank you" for all they have done for the family.

- Try to include items relating to your family history. Be sure to remind relatives to pass along to you any family history information, photos, documents, etc.

- Be as intimate as possible, within the boundries of good taste. Remember, your readers mean a great deal to you.

- Sign and date each newsletter.

## Family Reunion

In recent years the family reunion tradition has waned. I strongly recommend that you do everything in your power to revive this forgotten festivity. A family reunion is a great way for young and old to come together, at least for a day. People tell stories and can get a much better sense of where and from whom they have come. Human bonds are formed. For the family historian, a reunion is a wonderful time to interview, photograph and/or film family members, especially those who live long distances away.

These ideas will help you to organize and have a great family reunion:

- Ask for help from other family members. Don't try to do everything yourself.

- Try to include as many people, especially out of towners, as possible. Notify people as far in advance as possible when the reunion's exact date(s) will be. (I recommend at least six months.)

- Try to hold the reunion in the summer or fall, particularly around a holiday. You'll probably have better weather, and more people are able to travel because of vacations during those months.

- Have a group photograph taken, as well as family member photos.

- Set up a display of family heirlooms or historical photographs. Encourage relatives to bring their heirlooms and pictures to show and share.

- Ask people to update their address and telephone numbers.

- Have handouts relating to your family's history. Encourage family members to bring new information.

- During the reunion, try to set the date(s) for the next get together.

A family reunion can be a big project. Tom Ninkovich and Barbara Brown have published a comprehensive book on the subject, *Family Reunion Handbook: A Guide To Family Reunion Planning* ($14.95, Reunion Research). Topics they cover include getting others interested, site selection, and children's activities.

**Other Ideas**

There are many other ways to communicate within and among families. Your family may already be doing some now. Whenever you can, take the initiative and communicate. It doesn't have to be complex or expensive— send Christmas cards with a personal note; circulate announcements of important family events, such as births and deaths; have a "chain" where each person adds a little note and sends the entire letter on to the next family member on the list.

The possibilities are endless. Getting started, *taking action*, is up to you.

## Holiday Memories

Keeping in touch with family members is particularly important during holidays. As times change and pressures increase, the high-touch family must work hard to celebrate holidays together.

Traditions are an important part of family holidays. These are the ties that bind families together. They enhance family identity, create new closeness and promote stability. Traditions make the memories we carry with us for the rest of our lives.

It's important and fun to honor current family traditions and create new ones. While your family might not be a stand-in for a Norman Rockwell painting, a special family closeness is created when you celebrate holiday traditions together.

Keep these points in mind regarding family traditions:

- Simpler is better. Time consuming or complicated traditions usually don't last.

- Have traditions that focus on values and people, rather than on gifts or "things."

- One idea keeping very much in tune with the theme of this book is to adopt a tradition from your ancestor's homeland. When doing this, your family will feel a stronger bond with those who have gone before.

- Don't feel like you have to "manufacturer" new traditions. Many just seem to happen, rather than having to be contrived.

- Don't introduce too many new traditions at once. Wait until one or two new traditions are firmly established before beginning others. Too much change, too quickly, can overwhelm family members.

- Be flexible. Traditions, like most things in life, never go quite the way we expect. If something new works better, go for it.

- Be sure to pass on family traditions to younger family members by telling them and showing them what is involved. A tradition that stops is not a tradition.

Following are ideas that can enhance family participation and enjoyment during specific celebrations.

## New Year's Day

I love New Year's Day. It's a great time to both reflect on the past year and to plan (i.e., dream!) about the coming one.

Here are some ways you can make New Year's Day special:

- With your family, remember and honor in some way those relatives and special friends who died during the previous year.

- Record in a special place: where each member of your family lives; what they are doing at this time (working, going to school, etc.); and special events that are scheduled to take place in the coming year (a wedding, a fiftieth wedding anniversary, etc.). Have each family member present sign this.

- Brainstorm with family members to come up with one or two family goals for the coming year.

- Set aside some time to be by yourself. Take a walk. Contemplate your life's goals. Remember fun family times. Commit to something or someone. Resolve to take action.

## Memorial Day

For most people Memorial Day is an excuse for a three-day weekend and little else. But to the family member concerned with honoring those who gave "the last full measure of devotion," it is much more.

The most obvious way to enhance your Memorial Day celebration is to visit a cemetery where one or more family members are buried. Make a difference: leave some fresh flowers, do minor maintenance to the headstone (such as brushing away dirt and grass), clean up the surrounding landscape.

Most of all, pay tribute to relatives who have passed from this earth, regardless of whether they belonged to the armed services. These departed ancestors are a part of your family's heritage, culture and values. Honor them and thank them.

## Mother's and Father's Day

Mother's Day and Father's Day are wonderful times to tell special people that you love and care about them. Create your own traditions around these two days. Try to avoid the clichés: store-bought cards, flowers, ties too ugly to wear. Strive to be original, heartfelt and generous.

These are also days to pay tribute, in some way, to your grandparents. Let them know you care about them, their life, and their past; it will make them feel special.

## Fourth of July

At least some of your family's Fourth of July traditions should focus on paying tribute to our nation and its history. Especially if you have young children, this is an excellent time to learn more about our country's past and the relatives who lived through and experienced that past.

## Halloween

Many people shy away from Halloween because of its demonic overtones and graphic violence. In my family, we try hard to keep the fun of Halloween, without the scary, supernatural overtones. For example, the last three Halloweens my daughter has been a pumpkin, a mouse and Barney, the television dinosaur star.

Making your own, safe, Halloween traditions is important. Feel free to experiment and don't worry if you stray from the scariness.

One way to pay homage to the past during Halloween is to dress up in clothing from a certain time period. The Civil War, the Roaring 20's and the 1950's all invoke in our minds certain styles of clothing. Exposing our children to these times will give them a better feel for the time—and the people living then.

## Thanksgiving

Thanksgiving and Christmas are holidays that probably have the most established traditions.

Keep your Thanksgiving traditions simple and, whenever possible, focused on the blessings you and your family have received in the previous year. Here are several Thanksgiving tradition ideas:

- Share the cooking. Having too many cooks can spell trouble, but so can having too few.

- Call one person you used to know well but have not spoken with in many months. Tell them you are thinking about them and wish them well.

- Before beginning your Thanksgiving dinner, have a family member offer a toast. No matter how schmaltzy, as long as its heartfelt and warm, it will work.

- Foods can be traditions, too. Establish one or two dishes as traditions that you serve every Thanksgiving.

- Remember those less fortunate than you. Help the needy in some way.

- Either with your family or alone, write down as many things that you are thankful for as you can think of. Be sure to sign, date and keep this.

---

**♦ NOTE:**
**Some of my most memorable family traditions are the silliest. My grandmother used to finish each Thanksgiving meal by saying, "Oh, I'm full as a tick." To this day I'm not sure what she meant, but each time she said it, the grandkids would howl with laughter. It's as much a part of our family's Thanksgiving celebration as a turkey dinner.**

---

## Christmas Traditions

The magic and spirit of Christmas make it one of the best holidays for carrying out established family traditions, as well as creating new ones. What is for some a rushed, "thing" filled holiday can turn into a festive, meaningful family celebration.

What are some family Christmas traditions? The following are a few of the Christmas traditions that abound in one form or another:

- Lightening advent candles

- Having an advent calendar

- Making home-made Christmas cards, cookies and small gifts

- Chopping down a live Christmas tree

- Stringing cranberries and popcorn for the Christmas tree

- Going Christmas caroling

- Attending a midnight, candlelight church service

- Serving particular foods during the Christmas feast

- Giving gifts or assistance to the needy

Another tradition I read about recently and plan to start with my family this coming Christmas is to make one home-made tree ornament each year, to remember an event that happened during the previous twelve months. Moving to a new location, a promotion, a birth, a death or any other significant event worth remembering and preserving can be "made" into a tree ornament. When doing this, be sure to date each ornament.

◆ **EXERCISE:**
**On the lines below, note several Christmas traditions that are important to your family:**
1. _____
2. _____
3. _____
4. _____
5. _____

**List three new traditions that you want to start this coming Christmas:**
1. _____
2. _____
3. _____

## Hanukkah-Christmas Celebrations

Hanukkah is an eight-day Jewish celebration that falls between early and mid-December. Traditionally Hanukkah has been a minor, though merry, family festival. It's only similarity to Christmas is that both take place in December. Because there are increasing numbers of Jewish-Christian marriages today, family traditions during these two celebrations can be muddled or inconsistent: often combining traditions from each does not honor either.

Two books available about Jewish-Christian marriages include *Hanukkah and Christmas at My House* by Susan Enid Gertz ($6.95, Willow & Laurel) and *Raising Your Jewish-Christian Child*, by Lee F. Gruzen ($10.95, Dodd, Mead). Check your library or bookstore for other titles.

◆ **CHAPTER 7** ◆

---

# Giving Gifts that Last a Lifetime

*What is it I uniquely have to offer? What do I wish to leave behind
here? What is the nature of the unique service I bring to the table?*
—*Peter Block*

It has been said before that the real measure in life is what you give, not what you receive. This is never more true than when your family is involved.

Giving gifts that last a lifetime is a unique challenge. Not only will the receiver enjoy the meaningful gift he or she receives, your gift is likely to create a permanent memory in the receiver's mind. Your gift, and thus you, will live as long as that person lives.

How should *gift* be defined? I have always thought of a gift as something a person would love to have and enjoy, but for a myriad of reasons probably wouldn't buy for themselves. Your goal as a gift giver is to find that special gift, that special way of creating a forever memory, for a special person.

Giving gifts also allows you to give something back, be it to family, friends or society. In this chapter, you'll learn ways you can give something back in exchange for the many good graces you have received over time.

## Gifts with Meaning

Giving a simple gift can be a simple act. Giving a gift with meaning—something special that will be remembered, used and enjoyed for years and years to come—is more difficult.

This is particularly true when giving gifts to kids. It's easy to find something they'll like. Go into any toy store; the aisles will be jam-packed with dolls, trucks, games and hundreds of other items. You almost can't go wrong, provided you match the child's age with the recommended age range for the toy.

Giving a lasting gift requires more time and thought on your part. You'll have to hunt a little more, and make some extra efforts. But I am convinced your time and energy will be well spent when you find a great, meaningful, gift.

> *There are only two lasting bequests we can give*
> *our children—one is roots, the other is wings.*
> *— Anonymous*

## Engraved Gifts

Gifts with an inscription engraved on them make wonderful, lasting mementos. Giving something engraved shows you have taken the extra time and effort to give a special gift, and allows you to send a heartfelt message that will last for years.

What are some gifts that can be engraved? They can include, but are not limited to:

- Clocks
- Watches
- Jewelery—particularly lockets and bracelets
- Key chains
- Music boxes
- Pens
- Candlesticks
- Doorknockers
- Coffee mugs
- Beer mugs and other glasses
- Plates
- Books and albums

Check your local jewelery store to see if they offer engraving services. There are also stores dedicated to engraving gifts. One such national chain, located primarily in malls, is called Things Remembered. Call their toll-free telephone number for the location nearest you.

**Stamps**

United States postage stamps make excellent gifts to get kids excited about history. You may even start them on a lifelong hobby, for which they will always remember and thank you.

Your local post office is the place to begin to gather information about stamps. To receive their catalog, visit your local Post Office or write to:

- Philatelic Sales Division
  U.S. Postal Service
  Box 449997
  Kansas City, MO  64144-9997

Two special stamp programs are worth noting. The first allows you to receive every U.S. stamp issued during that year, cancelled with the First Day of Issue cancellation, for just $1.25 per page. Contact:

- Souvenir Pages Program
  Philatelic Sales Division
  United States Postal Service
  Box 44995
  Kansas City, MO  64144-9995

You also may be interested in receiving four or more mint stamps, along with a short history of the stamps. Each panel costs $4.95; they are mailed in groups of four, approximately every two months. Contact:

- Commemorative Panel Program
  Philatelic Sales Division
  United States Postal Service
  Box 449993
  Kansas City, MO  64144-9993

## Coins

Coin collecting is one of the world's oldest and largest hobbies. Like stamp collecting, it is a hobby that a person can enjoy throughout his or her entire life.

Coin collecting doesn't have to be expensive. Thousands of coins can be purchased for less than a dollar, with many good coins costing less than $10 each.

Visit a local coin shop for ideas. Great gifts include the excellent reference book by R.S. Yoeman entitled *A Guide Book To United States Coins*, a subscription to the weekly magazine *Coin World*, and a coin starter set that contains a variety of getting-started items. Several coin shop owners have told me that the new U.S. silver dollars, first released in 1986, make good gifts. They generally cost between $7-$8; because they were introduced so recently, a person can acquire a coin from each year for a relatively small investment.

## U.S. Savings Bonds

U.S. Savings Bonds make excellent gifts, especially when given to youngsters who one day will begin college and live on their own.

Basically, a savings bond is a contract that shows that the money used to purchase the bond has been loaned to the United States government, which promises to repay it, with accrued interest, when the bond is redeemed. Bonds are very safe investments because they are backed by the full faith and credit of the United States government, and they pay interest for up to 30 years.

You can purchase savings bonds in a variety of places. The most common is your local bank. Ask your employer if a payroll savings plan is available where savings bonds can be purchased automatically each month.

To obtain more detailed information about savings bonds, send a postcard with your name and address to:

- Office of Public Affairs
  Dept. P
  U.S. Savings Bonds Division
  Washington, D.C. 20226

## Other Financial Gifts

Consider giving a young child a piggy bank. This is a fun way to help children learn about money and saving. Be sure to include some change to get them started.

Another great gift would be to open a savings account at a bank in the child's name. You could make an initial deposit; it would be up to the child to add to the savings. Ask the bank if they will waive fees for children's accounts.

For big "kids," stocks are an investment tool that will, in all probability, grow over time; in the short term they offer benefits to the stockholders. For example, purchasers of Anheuser-Busch stock receive a 15 percent discount on admission to any of the nine Anheuser-Busch theme parks (which include Busch Gardens and Sea World). The Marriott Corporation offers breakfast and room discounts at its hotels, which include Residence Inns, Fairfield Inns and Courtyards. The Walt Disney Company gives discounts on lodging.

Buying stock doesn't have to be expensive because of broker's commissions. Many companies will let you buy stock directly from them. When buying stock, be sure to inquire about the company's Dividend Reinvestment Program, as well as opportunities to buy additional shares—sometimes for as low as $10 per investment.

## Local Artists

Local artists can be excellent resources for purchasing unique and meaningful gifts that are not found in traditional stores. Jewelry, paintings, pottery, rugs, Christmas ornaments, beadwork, basketry, weaving, recordings and clothes are some of the items that lend themselves to one-of-a-kind creations by talented people.

Your town or area might be famous for a particular product, which would make a great gift. Located near my parents' house in Lexington, Kentucky, is a local pottery company called Bybee Pottery. On the days Bybee opens its doors to customers, long lines of people clamor to get in; most of the products are gone within hours of opening the door.

## Games

Games make excellent gifts: they last a long time and are wonderful for creating memories when family members play together.

My family played board and card games of all kinds—I have many fond memories of those times. (We didn't *play* Monopoly,$^{TM}$ we *waged* Monopoly.$^{TM}$) Even today at our family gatherings, we almost always play some kind of game.

Games that make good gifts include chess, cribbage, checkers, cards, backgammon and board games such as Monopoly.™ It also is possible to purchase games associated with history, such as ones about the Civil War.

Two games related to family history are LifeStories, where players discuss their past experiences, and Futurestories, where players talk about their hopes and dreams. Created by LifeStories, Inc., both games retail for $29.95. Check your local toy store or contact LifeStories directly.

## Autographs

Autographs can be a fun and interesting gift that more often than not have strong historical ties. Think how much fun it would be to give (or have!) an autograph from Robert E. Lee, John F. Kennedy, Joe Louis, Amelia Earhart or scores of other historical figures.

Profiles in History specializes in buying and selling autographs. As of this writing, you can obtain six issues of their catalog for $35. Another source of quality autographs are the speciality stores now sprouting up that are devoted to autographs, particularly those related to sports and sports memorabilia. Check your phone book for stores near you.

## Framed Items

As I mentioned earlier, there's a special place in my heart for giving—and receiving—gifts that have been framed. These usually are pictures or prints. Framing a special item is an ideal way to make sure it is preserved for many years.

Framing isn't limited to pictures and artwork. Other items that look wonderful in frames include postcards, jerseys, baseball cards, magazines, programs, and needlepoint. The only limits are your creativity and your imagination.

## Books

I am a big fan of giving books as gifts, for two reasons. First, you can give a title that either the recipient is interested in or one that you would like them to become exposed to. Secondly, you can write a message inside the book to create a lasting record of your gift.

---

♦ **NOTE:**
**This is one good book to give as a gift! For additional copies, visit your local bookstore or write to the address shown at the back.**

---

## General Gifts

Not all gifts have to have a special or "deep" meaning. Following are some ideas for fun gifts that still have a personal touch:

- Specialized coffee mugs and T-shirts
- Personalized or special Christmas ornaments
- Motivational tapes
- Books on tapes
- Videos, especially those of a series, such as Ken Burns' PBS Series, *The Civil War*
- Inspirational calendars
- Luggage
- Regular or personalized stationary
- Watches
- Special coffees and coffee items
- Special food items—chocolate is the ultimate!
- Maps, globes or travel books
- Model airplanes, ships, cars
- Model railroads
- Cooking and kitchen items
- Posters or framed pictures
- PVC-free photo albums

Again, the most memorable or treasured gifts are often those you make yourself. These can be anything from canned tomatoes to personalized t-shirts. Your local arts and crafts store would be a good place to get ideas for gifts to make yourself. Get creative, make something you would enjoy receiving, and have fun!

## Gifts to Society

Giving gifts to family and friends can be very gratifying. Giving something to society can be even more rewarding.

Noted author and Nobel prize winner Elie Wiesel has said that giving something back to society is one of the mainstays of his life. "This guiding principle is the realization that what I receive I must pass on to others," Wiesel states. "I feel the need to pay back what was given to me."

Once again, your gifts to society can be as little or as much as your interest and resources permit. Obviously, there are many ways to give something back to society. The two main items you can give are your time and money. Hopefully, the following suggestions will stimulate more ideas on your part.

### Donate Money

Many worthwhile organizations need donations to sustain their efforts. Your contributions, regardless of the amount, can make a difference.

Obvious organizations you can donate money to are your local library, your church and your local schools. As previously mentioned, libraries are experiencing severe budget cutbacks that shrink services provided, hours of operation, and the number of new books purchased. For example, the city of San Francisco is currently involved in a tremendous effort to raise money for a new main library in the city's downtown. The vast majority of the money needed for the new building must come from private sources.

Other worthwhile donations include preserving the wilderness, furthering an educational institution (normally your alma mater) and for medical research (such as cancer research). Museums and the arts also are in desparate need of support.

Your donations do not have to be large. In 1993, the United States Holocaust Musuem, located in Washington, D.C., was opened through mostly private funding. For as little as a $25 donation, you can become a member and contribute to its upkeep.

You don't have to donate just *your* money, either. Many businesses will match your donations to charitable causes. You can also attempt to have others donate or match your contributions.

Remember, you can and will make a difference.

## Find a Cause

The alternative to donating money is to donate your time. Once again, the opportunities available for you to make a difference are almost limitless.

Schools, churches and libraries all rely on volunteers to make their organizations most effective. State and local governments also have numerous programs that rely on volunteers to feed the hungry, tutor the illiterate, shelter the homeless and counsel the distressed. Check the phone book or contact your local city or county government for information on volunteer opportunities available to you.

Three of the many national organizations that require local support include the Sierra Club, which educates and enlists people to maintain and/or restore the quality of the environment, City Harvest, which distributes surplus food from restaurants to soup kitchens and other hunger-relief agencies, and AMFAR (American Foundation for AIDS Research), which is the nation's leading nonprofit organization dedicated to the support of AIDS research.

I am interested in and support the Amyotrophic Lateral Sclerosis (ALS) Association. ALS, also known as Lou Gehrig's Disease, currently has doctors baffled—the cause, cure or means of control of this disease that strikes more than 5,000 new persons in the U.S. each year are presently unknown.

The really ambitious might consider joining the Peace Corps. For more than twenty-five years, Peace Corps volunteers have traveled the world, assisting developing areas with programs to promote health, agriculture, business and education. While once reserved for the young, many volunteers are now age fifty years and older. Check your phone book or contact your local Congressional representative for the Peace Corps office nearest you.

---

**♦ NOTE:**
**Find a cause that interests you, that you can get *passionate* about, and commit your time and energy. You'll be glad you did.**

---

## Gifts to the Unborn or Just-Born

The birth of a child is a special occasion. Honor both the child and the parents with special gifts.

One way to note the birth of a newborn is to place a classified ad in the local newspaper. This can then be clipped out, saved and shared for years.

Another idea is to create a time capsule for the child, filled with items related to the day he or she was born. Items appropriate for the time capsule can include the following:

- Local newspaper
- National newspaper(s)
- Weekly news magazine(s)
- Weekly sports magazine(s)
- Almanac and atlas
- Letters written by family members and friends
- Other selected magazines on various topics, such as science, religion, the arts, etc.

You'll find a more extensive discussion of time capsules in Chapter 2, "Preserving the Present." Two organizations that provide time capsules for infants include NU Born Time Capsules in Fremont, California, and The Original Time Capsule Company located in Greenfield, Indiana.

## Gifts to the Departed

In addition to paying your last respects to a departed loved one by attending their funeral or memorial service, you may want to pay a special tribute to them and their life with a gift. This can be an excellent way for you to turn your grief into something positive.

### Paid Obituary

A newspaper obituary provides one way to preserve a part of a person's life for future generations. Call the local newspaper and find out how to place an obituary. Most likely these will be paid obituaries, and that's fine: the cost will be relatively minor, compared to the lasting tribute and life record that results.

If you are unable to place an obituary, you can publish a similar record by buying a classified or regular ad. These will probably cost slightly more than an obituary, but will be well worth your investment.

When preparing the information, be sure to double check all facts and statements for accuracy. A mistake here could be passed on for generations and generations to come.

### New or Repaired Headstone

Many of your ancestors will have passed away fifty or sixty or more years before you were born. In some cases, when visiting their graves you will find that their headstone has been damaged, destroyed or was never dedicated in the first place. Contact the cemetery office to learn the procedures for replacing or repairing a headstone. Be sure to inquire about costs. Most cemeteries will be more than willing to assist your efforts.

Once again, when creating a new headstone, take all steps necessary to verify and check dates and statements. You are creating a permanent record. Be accurate with your information.

### Plaques or Monuments

One way to honor someone is with a plaque or a monument placed in a public place for all to see. This idea can be something simple, like a 12-inch square plaque placed next to a park bench, or expensive, such as a new science lab at the honoree's college alma mater.

Make the plaque or monument classy, understated and durable enough to last for years. This is another time to pay more for good quality.

## Plant a Tree

One of the most ecological gifts you can give a person is to plant a tree in their honor. Famous and Historic Trees, located in Jacksonville, Florida, specializes in providing trees for planting.

Famous Trees offers a wide range of tree varieties from which to choose, including: Mount Vernon Red Maple, Dwight D. Eisenhower Green Ash, Walden Woods River Birch, Robert E. Lee Black Locust, and Valley Forge Kentucky Coffeetree.

Most trees cost between $35 and $50 and come with instructions on how to plant and care for them. Each tree also comes with a personalized Certificate of Authenticity that includes space to record who planted the tree, where it was planted, and in whose memory the tree was planted to honor.

For an even more special tribute, you can place a plaque next to the tree, describing and honoring the person.

---

♦ **NOTE:**
**An added benefit of using Famous and Historic Trees' products is that a portion of the proceeds from every purchased tree is donated to the The Civil War Trust.**

---

# PART 4

## Finding Your Family History

# CHAPTER 8

# Family Research Basics

*The highest and most powerful motivation in doing
(family history research) is not for ourselves only, but for our posterity,
for the posterity of all mankind.*
—Stephen R. Covey

*You can't possibly know where you're going
if you don't know where you've been.*
—Ken Burns

If you've made it this far with me, by now you must have realized my passion about both preserving the present and researching one's family's past. No other undertaking has taught me more about myself than researching my family history. I strongly recommend you try to learn at least a little more about your family's past.

This chapter will give you a preliminary introduction to family history research. It is not meant to be a comprehensive guide, just a starting point; there are scores of books written on the subject of researching your family history.

Your efforts don't have to be fancy or extensive. You can do as little or as much as you like in virtually any form or format. I recommend that you start by seeing where your interests lie, and then following them.

I will offer one warning: be careful—family history research can be addicting. I certainly have the bug.

## Some How-To's

Family research is a lot of fun. You have to be part detective, historian, writer, researcher and many other things. I often say doing family history research is like putting a jigsaw puzzle together; the added challenge is that one must first find the pieces of the puzzle before connecting them.

I recommend the following seven-point plan to begin your family research.

1. *Find a family tree form that makes it easy to record data about an individual or family.* Most genealogy societies have these forms readily available. Check your local library for the society closest to you. Many books available in the library or at bookstores contain family tree research forms that you can copy or they will suggest places to purchase forms.

2. *Work backwards from the known to the unknown.* Start with yourself and fill out as much information as you can about your life. Do the same with your parents, grandparents and so on.

3. *Talk to all of your living relatives and continue to fill-in information on your family record sheets.* Talk to all of your relatives and ask them questions about the family. Start with their life and then move on to common relatives' lives.

   During this phase, you will probably receive a great deal of information. Record it all; later you can arrange and rearrange. You will probably discover that some of the information contradicts other information. For example, one aunt might say your grandfather was born on June 10, 1906; another aunt might say he was born on June 6, 1910. Remember, memories can play tricks.

   When interviewing relatives, pay particular attention to determining *where* a person was born or died. Once you confirm this information, you can write to the appropriate county courthouse and obtain a birth or death certificate (see step 4).

   At this time, ask for photos of each of your relatives. As you become involved in your research, you will want to know everything about a person, including what they looked like.

◆ **EXERCISE:**
**List eight relatives who you think would have information about**
**your family. Once you've spoken with the person, record the date.**

| NAME | DATE |
|---|---|
| 1. _____ | _____ |
| 2. _____ | _____ |
| 3. _____ | _____ |
| 4. _____ | _____ |
| 5. _____ | _____ |
| 6. _____ | _____ |
| 7. _____ | _____ |
| 8. _____ | _____ |

4.   *Prove what you have been told by documented evidence.* Up to now, you
     have compiled what is known as an oral history. Someone has told
     information to you, but you have little, if any, physical proof. Some
     people may be content to record this information, accept it as valid,
     and never verify the information's accuracy. I recommend proving the
     information you have been told via records and other documentation.

     Again, utilizing yourself and your relatives, ask for and gather as
     many copies of documents (birth and death certificates, school records,
     and so on) as possible. You will quickly learn that these documents
     contain a wealth of information about a person.

     Once you have obtained copies of all documents in your and your
     family's possession, you will want to locate copies of missing records.
     The key is to write to the county courthouse where the event took
     place. For example, let's say your grandfather was born in Sabina,
     Ohio. By looking at a map of Ohio, you determine that Sabina is
     located in Clinton County. Further research shows the county seat of
     Clinton County is a town called Washington Courthouse. You could
     then write to the Clinton County Courthouse in Washington Court-
     house and request a copy of your grandfather's birth certificate.

---

♦  **NOTE:**
**Include a self-addressed, stamped envelope when writing for
family records. If the courthouse does not have the information
you request, they will usually let you know where the records are
and how to obtain copies.**

---

5.   *Reexamine the information you have collected to date, then focus on obtaining
missing pieces.* Here is where you'll want to regroup a bit and determine
exactly what information you have been told, what information you
have documented records, and what information you would like to
obtain. Please note that it is fairly easy to quickly get overwhelmed
with paper, names, dates, records and the like when beginning a family
history project. Now would be a good time to devise some sort of information filing system that you are comfortable using.

6.   *Utilize other research sources.* Once you obtain information from the two
main sources—relatives and county courthouses—you can begin to
utilize other sources for possible clues about your ancestors. These can
include church records, census records, cemetery gravestones (be sure
to obtain caretaker records) and family Bibles (see the following page
for more ideas). Even something as simple and basic as exploring attics
can lead to the discovery of many genealogical treasures.

7.   *Write what you have and give copies to family members and friends.* Your
research will not be complete, but periodically you will want to record
and share the information you have obtained. Your relatives will certainly enjoy reading about your discoveries and, hopefully, this will
encourage them to offer additional information.

Once you complete these seven steps, you will be well on your way to creating
a valuable family history. Later, depending on your interest and time, you may
want to consider more advanced endeavors, such as hiring a professional
genealogist to do additional research, or traveling to Salt Lake City to visit the
Mormon Church's genealogy files. (The Church of Jesus Christ of Latter-day Saints,
or Mormon Church, has the largest collection of family records in the world. Both
church members and non-members can conduct research at the main library, or at
the church's more than 2,000 "family history centers" located across the country.)

## People and Places to Research

Starting from scratch to learn information about a person can be daunting. Early in my research efforts, I looked at my share of blank record forms and asked myself, "Where do I begin?"

Investigate the following to find information about someone:

- Your relatives
- Family scrapbooks and photo albums
- Friends and schoolmates of your relatives
- Libraries
- Cemeteries
- County court houses
- Churches
- The National Archives and state archives
- Census records
- Wills and Probate records
- Tax records
- Social Security records
- Newspapers, especially obituaries
- Land records
- Immigrant passenger lists
- Military records
- Historical societies and genealogy organizations
- City directories
- Published genealogies
- City, county and state histories

Traces of your ancestors' lives can be found in many different places. Serious family history researchers investigate as many sources as possible.

## Final Thoughts

By now you have a basic blueprint to start researching your family history. I recommend spending some time doing preliminary research. See if you get excited about it. If you want to continue, there are many books and other resources that can help you become more proficient at tracking down the lives of your relatives. Check your local library or bookstore for help in locating appropriate books (several are mentioned in the section "Related Books Worth Reading").

If you do get the bug, you will become involved in a challenging, rewarding hobby that can last a lifetime. I've discovered that the more information I find about a person, the more questions I develop; in other words, the challenge never ends.

In addition to being a great gift to family and friends, researching the past is a way of paying tribute to the men and women of your family who have come—and gone—before you.

---

# Quick-Start Steps to Beginning

*In life, lots of people know what to do, but few people actually*
*do what they know. Knowing is not enough. You must take action.*
*—Anthony Robbins*

## A Recap

This book's central theme believes your life is unique, and it's up to you to save and share parts of it with this and future generations. Numerous ideas are presented regarding ways to preserve and enhance parts of your life.

Remember, you don't have to do everything. Pick and choose the ideas that interest you. Even doing a few of the suggestions will be worthwhile.

To simplify things a little, the following page offers one way to proceed. You can, of course, use this as as guide or do other ideas that appeal more to you.

## Do It Today

Regardless of how old you are or how much free time you have, you can and must begin your preservation efforts *today*. Author and motivational speaker Tony Robbins says each of us has the "ability to take action." Just reading this book won't preserve parts of your life; you must be willing to take action.

## Enjoy

Once you get started, it is important to remember to enjoy your preservation efforts. Have fun with this. Think of all the joy and entertainment you will provide family members and friends in the years to come. Enjoy your preservation journey.

## Level 1

- Buy and keep a folder or envelope for important papers and other items (page 10).

- Purchase a family Bible and record important family-related dates and events (page 13).

- Sort, label and put into photo-safe albums existing photographs (page 34).

## Level 2

- Begin a journal or other blank book project (pages 58 and 62).

- Create a video heirloom using new and existing video (page 43).

- Begin writing your family history (page 70).

## Level 3

- Plan a family reunion within the next year (page 89).

- Begin writing your autobiography (page 64).

- Purchase a time capsule, fill it with mementos, and have it sealed and safely stored (page 22).

# Organizations Mentioned in This Book

## Genealogy

Family History Library
The Church of Jesus Christ of Latter-day Saints
35 Northwest Temple Street
Salt Lake City, UT 84150
(801) 240-2331

National Genealogical Society
4527 17th Street North
Arlington, VA 22207
(703) 525-0050

## Gifts

Famous & Historic Trees
8555 Plummer Road
Jacksonville, FL 32219
(800) 677-0727

Profiles in History
345 N. Maple Dr., Ste. 202
Beverly Hills, CA 90210
(800) 942-8856

Coin World
P.O. Box 150
Sidney, OH 45365
(513)-498-0800

## Miscellaneous

Exposures
1 Memory Lane, P.O. Box 3615
Oshkosh, WI 54903-3615
(800) 222-4947

LifeStories, Inc.
701 Decatur Avenue North, Suite 104
Golden Valley, MN 55427
(800) 232-1873

Mary Lou Productions
P.O. Box 17233
Minneapolis, MN 55417
(612) 726-9432

Reunion Research
3145 Geary Blvd., #14
San Francisco, CA 94118
(209) 336-2345

Show Video Gifts
6790 Main Street
Williamsville, NY 14221
(800) 523-0006

Things Remembered
5340 Avion Park Drive
Cleveland, OH 44143
Call (800) 274-7367 for the location nearest you

Thomas Nelson Publishers (blank books)
Nelson Place
Nashville, TN 37214
(800) 251-4000

Walter's Cookbooks
215 5th Aveneu S.E.
Waseca, MN  56093
(800) 447-3274

## Preservation

The Association for the Preservation of Civil War Sites
613 Caroline St., Suite B
Fredericksburg, VA  22401
(703) 371-1860

The Civil War Trust
1225 Eye Street, N.W.
Washington, D.C. 20005
(202) 326-8420

Creative Memories
2815 Clearwater Road
St. Cloud, MN 56302
(800) 468-9335

Kemper and Leila Williams Foundation
The Historic New Orleans Collection
533 Royal Street
New Orleans, LA  70130
(504) 523-4662

Light Impressions
P.O. Box 940
Rochester, NY  14603
(800) 828-6216

National Trust for Historic Preservation
1785 Massachusetts Ave., N.W.
Washington, D.C. 20036
(202) 673-4175

The Preservation Emporium
2600 Stemmons Freeway, Suite 131
Dallas, TX  75207
(800) 442-2038

## Time Capsules

Erie Landmark Company
4449 Brookfield Corporate Drive
Chantilly, VA  22021-1681
(800) 874-7848

International Time Capsule Society (ITCS)
c/o Oglethorpe University
4484 Peachtree Road, N.E.
Atlanta, GA  30319
(404) 364-8446

NU Born Time Capsules
2478 Harrisburg Avenue
Fremont, CA  94536
(800) 868-2676

The Orginial Time Capsule Company
5859 West U.S. Highway 40
Greenfield, IN  46140
(800) 729-8463

## Volunteer Opportunities

AMFAR (American Foundation for AIDS Research)
733 Third Avenue
New York, NY  10017
(800) 39-AMFAR

The Amyotrophic Lateral Sclerosis Association
21021 Ventura Blvd., Ste. 321
Woodland Hills, CA  91364
(818) 340-7500

City Harvest, Inc.
159 West 25th Street
New York, NY 10001
(212) 463-0456


The National VOLUNTEER Center
1111 North 19th Street, Suite 500
Arlington, VA 22209
(800) 755-6882


Neighborhood Reinvestment Corporation
1325 G. St., N.W.
Suite 800
Washington, D.C. 20005
(202) 376-2400


The Sierra Club
730 Polk Street
San Francisco, CA 94109
(800) 935-1056


United States Holocaust Memorial Museum
100 Raoul Wallenberg Place, SW
Washington, D.C. 20024-2150
(202) 488-0400

# Related Books Worth Reading[7]

The following books have influenced me in some way and/or share some common thread with this book. Enjoy.

Biffle, Christopher. *A Journey Through Your Childhood*. Los Angeles: Jeremy P. Tarcher, Inc., 1989.

Bradbury, Ray. *Dandelion Wine*. New York: Doubleday, 1957.

Braham, Barbara. *Finding Your Purpose*. Menlo Park, CA: Crisp Publications, 1991.

Buscaglia, Leo. Just about anything he has written.

Chapman, E. N. *Attitude: Your Most Priceless Possession*. Menlo Park, CA: Crisp Publications, 1990.

Collins, Gary R. *You Can Make a Difference* (audio). Grand Rapids, MI: Zondevan, 1992.

Covey, Stephen R. *The 7 Habits of Highly Effective People*. New York: Simon & Schuster, 1989.

Evans, Fanny-Maude. *Changing Memories into Memoirs*. New York: Barnes & Noble Books, 1984.

Gertz, Susan. *Hanukkah & Christmas at My House*. Middleton, Ohio: Willow & Laurel, 1992.

Gruzen, Lee. *Raising Your Jewish/Christian Child*. New York: Dodd, Mead, 1987.

Haley, Alex. *Roots*. Garden City, NY: Doubleday & Company, Inc., 1976.

Hembold, F. Wilbur. *Tracing Your Ancestry*. Birmingham, AL: Oxmoor House, 1976.

Mann, Thomas. *Buddenbrooks*. New York: Vintage Books, 1984.

Ninkovich, Tom and B. Brown. *Family Reunion Handbook*. San Francisco: Reunion Research, 1992.

Simons, George. *Keeping Your Personal Journal*. New York: Ballantine Books, 1978.

Shull, Wilma Sadler. *Photographing Your Heritage*. Salt Lake City: Ancestry, 1988.

Stegner, Wallace. *Angle of Repose*. New York: Penguin Books, 1971.

—— *The Big Rock Candy Mountain*. New York: Penguin Books, 1943.

Steinback, John. *Travels with Charley*. New York: Viking Press, 1962.

[7]In my opinion

Stoddard, Alexandra. *Gift of A Letter*. New York: Avon Books, 1991.

——*Living a Beautiful Life*. New York: Avon Books, 1988.

Westin, Jeane Eddy. *Finding Your Roots*. New York: Ballantine Books, 1977.

Woolf, Virginia. *Moments of Being*. San Diego: Harcourt Brace Jovanovich, 1985.

X, Malcom, with Alex Haley. *The Autobiography of Malcolm X*. New York: Ballatine Books, 1989.

Yalom, Marilyn and Susan Bell. *Revealing Lives: Autobiography, Biography, and Gender*. Albany, NY: State University of New York Press, 1990.

Yoeman, R.S. *A Guide Book To United States Coins*. Racine, WI: Western, 1991.

Zimmerman, Bill. *How to Tape Instant Oral Biographies*. New York: Bantam Books, 1992.

# Acknowledgements

Many people, both directly and indirectly, played a role in producing this book. I would like to thank them all, especially:

——My wife Gyoconda and daughter Alexandra, who are my support and inspiration. They make me want to preserve a place in their hearts and history.

——My "Board of Advisors" who contributed extensively from concept to completion: Bill Kaufmann, Diana West and Bob Will.

——Jeff Holmes, who designed the cover, and Michele Smith, who contributed the illustrations found inside the book. Both helped me focus and enhance the material through their creativity.

——Bev Manber, who edited the manuscript in all the right places.

——The "interviewees" who gave their time and ideas: John Gowan, Paula Julianel, Dr. George Simons, Michele Smith, and Marilyn Yalom.

——The review team who read all or part of the manuscript at one point or another and provided valuable feedback: Steve and Erika Mitchell, Nancy Sallan, Mary Ann Burke, David and Sonja Marcus, Erik "Go Mets" Marcus, Elwood Chapman, and Mary Jo Henricksen.

——Mike Crisp, both for his support of my efforts and his everyday example of a creative, successful publisher.

——The CPI editorial team of Kathleen Barcos, Karla Nguyen and Susan Bagley, who guided me and answered my questions.

# About the Author

Tim Polk has been avidly researching his family history and preserving parts of his life for more than ten years. His quest for information has taken him throughout the United States and Europe. Author of a 150-page family history entitled *Our Family Present and Past*, he lives in Sunnyvale, California, with his wife and daughter.

# Index

# Order Form

To order copies of this book, contact your local bookstore or use this order form.

## SHIP TO

Name: _____

Street Address: _____

City: _____State: _____ Zip:_____

Telephone number (required):_____

## ORDERING INFORMATION

Please send me _____ copies of *How to Outlive Your Lifetime*! at $10.95 each.

    Please include shipping charges (see below).

    Purchase 10 or more titles and receive a 10% discount.

    California residents please add 8.25% sales tax.

## METHOD OF PAYMENT

☐ Check or Money Order enclosed (make checks payable to Family Life)

☐ Charge my order to:    ☐ MasterCard   ☐ VISA

    Card No:_____

    Expiration date:_____

    Name on card:_____

    Authorized signature (required):_____

## SHIPPING

Please specify one option:

☐ Book rate (2-4 weeks): $2.00 first book, $.50 each additional book.

☐ Priority mail (2-4 days): $3.50 first book, $.75 each additional book.

☐ Air Mail: $3.50 per book

## TOTAL

Total for book(s), shipping, and sales tax (if applicable): _____

---

**SEND ORDERS TO:**

**Family Life International**
**P.O. Box 2803-01**
**Sunnyvale, CA 94087**

**OR CALL:**

**1-800-357-7772**
**(408) 730-0831**